Porcelain

repair and *restoration*

Porcelain

repair and *restoration*

Nigel Williams

SECOND EDITION

REVISED BY Loretta Hogan and Myrtle Bruce-Mitford

University of Pennsylvania Press
Philadelphia

First published 1983
Second edition first published 2002 by The British Museum Press

Second edition first published in the United States 2002 by
University of Pennsylvania Press
Philadelphia, Pennsylvania 19104-4011

A catalog record for this book is available from the Library of Congress

ISBN 0-8122-3703-X

Designed, edited, and produced by Hilton/Sadler

Typeset in Sabon
Printed in Italy by L.E.G.O. SpA

To Matty

Acknowledgements
We should like to extend our thanks to the following people: Dr W. A. Oddy, former Keeper of
Conservation in the British Museum, Sandra Smith, Acting Keeper of Conservation, and Sarah Watkins,
Head of Ceramics, Glass and Metals Conservation, for their help and encouragement; Trevor Springett
of the Photographic Department for all the photography; Claire Thorne for the line drawings; Patricia
Hamilton for producing the first typescript; Vivienne Tremain, Brenda Burr and Nina Whitmore for
further typing; Robert Knox, Keeper of Oriental Antiquities in the British Museum, and Jonathan
Mitchell for the loan of objects. We also acknowledge with gratitude the assistance of colleagues in
Ceramics, Glass and Metals Conservation – in particular, Denise Ling, Senior Conservation Officer;
Brenda Cannon, Conservation Administrator; scientists in the Conservation Research Group; and
Jessica Harrison-Hall, Assistant Keeper in the Department of Oriental Antiquities. Finally, we wish to
thank Ken Medwell at the Airbrush and Spray Centre in Worthing, Ken Watts, tutor at West Dean
College, and Wendy Walker, Assistant Conservator, and Anna Studebaker, Research Associate, at the
Metropolitan Museum, New York, for their helpful advice.

Contents

Foreword

Nigel Williams died of a heart attack on the beach at Aqaba, Jordan, on 21 April 1992. He was on a short break from working on a British Museum excavation at Tell es-Sa'idiyeh, where he was the on-site conservator. Nigel had served the British Museum all his working life after leaving the Central School of Arts and Crafts in 1961, and had become the Museum's most experienced conservator of ceramics and Head of the Ceramics and Glass Conservation Section in the Department of Conservation. His expertise had led to a number of invitations to lecture overseas and to advise museums on their conservation needs.

Nigel was also widely known as a teacher of ceramic conservation, both inside and outside the British Museum. This book, first published in 1983, was written not only for the benefit of his numerous students – in particular, those who came to his evening classes year after year – but also because there was at that time no authoritative book in print that expounded museum practice in ceramic restoration.

At the time of his death, Nigel had been working on a revised edition and it seemed at first that this task could not be completed. The style of the book was idiosyncratic, the copious revision notes were often difficult to follow, and the original illustrations could not be found. However, Myrtle Bruce-Mitford and Loretta Hogan accepted the task of bringing the second edition to fruition. Myrtle, a published author in her own right, was Nigel's partner for nearly twenty-five years and edited much of his writing; Loretta is a Senior Conservation Officer in the Ceramics, Glass and Metals Section of the Conservation Department at the British Museum and was a colleague of Nigel's for some eight years. It is a tribute to them that, thanks to their labours of love and dedication, the book is available again and that, in spite of considerable rewriting, in particular to take account of developments in techniques and materials since 1992, much of the style of the original has been preserved.

To those of us who had the privilege of knowing and working with Nigel, his first edition is an old friend with which we will never part. The second edition will ensure that his life's work lives on in that of his colleagues and students. The book was written as a practical, how-to-do-it guide for the ceramic restorer and I commend it to you heartily.

Dr W. A. Oddy
Former Keeper, Department of Conservation
The British Museum
Retired January 2002

Introduction

Books about porcelain restoration in the past have tended to imply that there is one way, and one way only, to restore porcelain. (The one notable exception, *China Mending and Restoration* by Parsons and Curl, is now sadly out of date.) A single-minded approach to any problem can, of course, have its benefits, and very often the well-trodden and proven path is the best one to take. The most frequently suggested method for restoring porcelain will, undoubtedly, be a sound one, but restoration and conservation are very much a matter of individual taste. The 'perfect' method advocated by one individual may be a cumbersome and excruciating process to another. Any left-handers among you who were painstakingly taught by their teachers to write with their right hands will know all too well what I mean.

In view of the wide range of materials that can be successfully used for porcelain restoration, it is perhaps surprising that very few of them are made with that end in mind. Hence, the endless yet often stimulating discussion among restorers as to which of the materials available are best, and which techniques employed result in the most perfect piece of restoration. Personal preference is more often than not at the heart of these discussions – my own pet hate, for example, is the use of an epoxy resin twin-pack as a filler. Although many restorers I know swear by such a product and use it all the time with very acceptable results, I have always found it difficult to cut and too soft and slippery to the touch.

My experience as both a teacher and a restorer of porcelain has taught me that expert results can, in fact, be achieved with a variety of techniques and materials. It is not, in other words, a matter of learning the correct method – there are many options open. Admittedly, success is much more likely if aspiring restorers use methods and materials with which they are thoroughly at home, rather than struggling with unfamiliar ones because they are fashionable or generally accepted. One of the purposes of this book, however, is to give novice porcelain restorers an informed understanding of other options, and thus to encourage them to discover, by reading and experiment, the techniques that best suit their approach to the task.

In the book, therefore, I shall discuss some of the many different adhesives, fillers and glazing mediums that can successfully be used to restore porcelain. It will then be up to you, the reader, to determine by practical application which materials and methods you prefer. On occasions, the object itself will dictate what you must use and how you should proceed.

Once you have found a method that suits you, do not change for the sake of it. Expertise in anything comes only with accumulated experience – and experience can be achieved only through familiarity with both materials and techniques. This is not to say that you should never experiment, but if you do try a new material or technique you should make sure that the long-term result is better than the result achieved with the method you are accustomed to using. In other words, do not abandon your tried and trusted technique until you are

Take note

It must be stressed that this book does not deal with the restoration of low-fired pottery: the methods and materials appropriate for restoring this type of pottery are very different from those needed for porcelain. Considerable damage may be caused if some of the materials and techniques described here are used on soft-bodied ceramic objects, whether they are glazed or unglazed.

absolutely certain that you have discovered a miraculous new method or a vastly superior new material.

You must always bear in mind that porcelain restoration is essentially a practical art and that only a certain amount can be learned through long hours spent in the library. I would, therefore, advise you to enrol in a class where you will be able to see and use the techniques for restoration described in this and other books on the subject. Once you have joined a class, you will benefit from the experience of other restorers and also cut down on your expenses. Some materials used in conservation are very expensive, and if you can share the financial burden – remembering that you will often require only small amounts of some of the most costly items – then so much the better.

Porcelain restoration is a logical process. There are six stages you may have to follow, depending on the damage the object has incurred:

1 Examination
2 Dismantling
3 Cleaning
4 Joining
5 Filling
6 Painting and glazing

BELOW The lower parts of the left-hand and central panels of this oriental vase have been restored, and the decoration partially completed.

Your preliminary examination of the item to be restored will tell you whether you can afford to miss out any of the five subsequent stages. Before starting any job, it is crucial to ascertain the exact requirements of the owner – one person may like to see where an object has been restored, for example, whereas another will insist that any restoration work be completely invisible.

Some people may consider it wrong for a restorer from a national museum to teach invisible restoration, perhaps feeling that certain unscrupulous dealers may profit from such a practice (as they may indeed do, for even an expert will sometimes find it very difficult to determine, without the aid of an ultraviolet lamp, whether a piece has been restored or not). I must emphasize, however, that I am not advocating the type of so-called 'restoration' whereby objects are bastardized to deceive a would-be buyer. I have seen far too many examples of pieces that have been hacked about almost to the point of destruction: the type of practice whereby the stubs of handles are ground away to transform the original piece into a finger-bowl; where vases with necks missing are cut down to bowls; where figures with arms and legs missing undergo transplants to convince would-be purchasers that they are looking at the original, undamaged object. This book will not teach you 'creative' restoration of the type intended to deceive. We cannot and should not turn our backs and hope that such practices will somehow disappear; what I can do, however, in the pages that follow is to show that if a piece is restored properly there will be no need to resort to undesirable measures of this kind. All the processes advocated here are reversible.

Many of the materials I discuss have been or are still being used in ceramic conservation at the British Museum. They will have been tested by the Conservation Research Group for various properties, including reversibility, ageing, discoloration, strength, compatibility with other materials and suitability for different types of ceramic before being passed as suitable for use on a Museum object. No particular brand of material is recommended by the British Museum as being more suitable for porcelain restoration than another. There are, indeed, many products on the market as well as new ones constantly being developed, some of which may meet all the requirements of the modern, professional porcelain restorer.

Health and safety

Before embarking on the various stages of porcelain restoration, you would be well advised to heed the following words of warning regarding the use of some of the specialist materials you are certain to come across. If these are not handled with care, they can be dangerous.

In the last few years not only has our use of synthetic resins increased but also our understanding of them and our awareness of the effect they can have on the user. Rules on the use of these resins at work have accordingly become much more stringent. Those porcelain restorers (the majority) who work in small shops or in rooms at home, should take the potential health risks attached to using these materials just as seriously as those who work in a museum laboratory or a large, commercial workshop. Attention to health and safety precautions should be of paramount importance wherever and whenever you are using a substance that can affect your health.

By law now anyone running a workshop, especially if responsible for others using chemicals, has to comply with the Control of Substances Hazardous to Health Regulations 1988 (COSHH). All chemicals and materials have to be assessed for levels of risk to health and safety. There is a limit to the quantity of resin or solvent that can safely be used at the bench over a period of time, and this limit is directly related to the cubic area in which the substance is being used. The COSHH assessment should state clearly the chemical name of each product, a job description, the hazard classification – for example, highly flammable – and the exposure risk, together with proposals for control measures to limit exposure and to provide personal protection. Data sheets for every chemical in use can be obtained on request from the manufacturers. These give precise details on each product, including composition, chemical properties, hazards and first-aid measures, handling and storage, exposure and personal protection levels, along with other useful information. These details can be used to estimate how dangerous the material is in order to apply the appropriate level of protection in line with COSHH regulations.

UK hazard symbols

Toxic
These substances present a serious risk of acute or chronic poisoning if inhaled, ingested or absorbed through the skin.

Oxidizing
These substances give rise to highly exothermic reactions when they come into contact with other substances, particularly flammable ones.

Corrosive
These substances will destroy living tissue.

UK hazard symbols

Flammable

Extremely flammable liquids have a flash-point less than 0°C (32°F) and a boiling point of 35°C (95°F) or less.

Highly flammable substances include:
Those that may become hot and finally catch fire in contact with air at ambient temperature without the application of energy.

Those that may readily catch fire after brief contact with a source of ignition and that continue to burn or to be consumed after the removal of the source of ignition.

Those that are gaseous and flammable in the air at normal pressure.

Those in contact with water or damp air that give off highly flammable gases in dangerous quantities.

Liquids that have a flash-point below 21°C (70°F).

Flammable liquids are those that have a flash-point in the range 21°C (70°F) to 55°C (131°F).

Risk assessments should also be carried out on all potentially hazardous equipment in the workshop; these would cover everything from the safe use of compressed air (*see p. 111*) to the use and safe disposal of sharp objects, such as scalpel blades. Finally, if you are responsible for the well-being of others in the workshop you need to train them in the safe use and handling of all potentially dangerous equipment and materials. Always label bottles and containers holding chemicals and materials clearly with their name and appropriate safety stickers (*shown on pp. 9–11*), such as toxic, flammable, corrosive and so on. Stickers should also be used to identify chemicals in use, such as a solvent left in a desiccator during treatment – you may know what it is, but someone else may not.

Here is a summary of the possible dangers to health and safety that may be encountered in restoring porcelain, together with a list of basic precautions that may reduce, though not remove, those dangers. I have restricted myself to the two areas that constitute the greatest, if not the only, risk to porcelain restorers – the use of resins and solvents and the hazard of fire.

Resin

The incorrect use of a resin may have a number of effects on the person handling it. Some of these will manifest themselves almost immediately – for example, irritation of the eyes caused by airborne fumes or by small droplets of resin while spraying. Other symptoms, such as skin rashes caused by the handling of epoxy or polyester resin, may build up gradually over a period of months or even years. More long-term effects may be caused by breathing in fumes from a polyester resin; inhaling large amounts will cause headaches and stomach pains that will return on each subsequent exposure to the fumes. I myself suffer from such a problem, though it was caused as a result not of restoring porcelain but of working for long periods with large quantities of this resin when I was building a boat.

From these examples it can be seen that some form of protection for the restorer is essential. This could, at its most basic level, take the form of just a set of overalls to protect your arms and clothes from spilled resins; at the other end of the scale, it could be an advanced form of fume extraction. I can only recommend that you buy the best possible safety apparatus you can afford. Ideally you should take the following measures:

1 Always wear protective overalls.
2 Whenever possible, wear protective gloves for mixing, applying and sanding resins.
3 Put a protective barrier cream on any areas of exposed skin.
4 Wear goggles when mixing liquid resins.
5 Always wear an appropriate dust and fume mask for sanding resins and working with solvents.
6 Remove resins spilled on any part of your body immediately.
7 Always spray resins in a spray booth or in an area with fume extraction; if you have only a ventilated room, wear an appropriate mask.

8 Large amounts of resin should be used only in fume cupboards or in a ventilated room; if you do not have a fume cupboard, it is essential that you wear an appropriate mask.

Nitrile gloves, which are disposable, are very useful because although protective they are thin enough to enable you to feel what you are doing.

Suitable dust masks made by 3M are numbers 8810, 8822 and 9913. For fumes, 3M 4277 is a suitable mask, as long as the organic vapour concentration is below 1000 ppm (parts per million); if it is greater than this figure you will have to work in a fume cupboard. Masks have a safe-use limit of only a few hours (how many should be indicated on the box), after which they will not be effective, so keep a careful check on how long you have used them. Store your mask in a sealed plastic bag to avoid contamination when not in use.

Goggles are used to protect your eyes from the hazards of dust and splashes from chemicals and resins. Check that the goggles you purchase comply with the relevant British and European standards.

Fire
The second greatest risk to a porcelain restorer is fire. Many of the solvents and thinners used are highly flammable. Of these, acetone, industrial methylated spirit (IMS) and cellulose thinners are the most dangerous of all; acetone, in particular, has a very low flash-point and is, therefore, potentially one of the most risky. Again, you can reduce the hazards greatly by following a few simple, common-sense measures:

1 Do not permit smoking in the workshop.
2 Never place large quantities of flammable liquid on work areas.
3 Keep flammable materials in a metal cupboard.
4 Keep flammable materials away from naked flame.
5 Keep flammable materials away from any electrical appliance that may spark.
6 Wipe up any spillage, allowing it to evaporate in a safe area.
7 Use narrow-necked bottles to store solvents.
8 Have fire-fighting equipment to hand: extinguishers, blankets and sand.
9 Make sure that all flammable chemicals are clearly labelled as such.

Finally, always have a well-stocked first-aid box, including an eye-wash bottle, readily accessible in the event of an accident.

Information regarding COSHH regulations and risk assessments can be obtained from HMSO Bookshop at 49 High Holborn, London WC1V 6HB.

Further information regarding health and safety aspects of chemicals can be found in *Chemicals in Conservation* (2nd edn), by Amanda Clydesdale, published in 1990 by the Conservation Bureau (ISBN 0 9508068 46).

UK hazard symbols

Harmful
These substances present a moderate risk to health if they are inhaled, ingested or absorbed through the skin.

Irritant
These substances are non-corrosive but are liable to cause inflammation if they come into immediate, prolonged or repeated contact with the skin or mucous membranes.

Sensitizing
These substances can cause immediate reactions, including rashes, headaches and nausea, in people repeatedly exposed to them in the past.

Carcinogenic
These substances can cause cancer if they are inhaled, ingested or absorbed through the skin.

1 The history of ceramic repair

The history of ceramic restoration is nearly as old as that of pottery itself. The earliest known repair in the British Museum – and this is certainly not the first – is about 7000 years old, and therefore for me to describe all the methods and materials that have ever been used would clearly be impossible.

If you have ever been on an excavation, or watched one of the many popular television programmes dealing with archaeology, you will know that it is not unusual to find considerable quantities of pottery and thousands of sherds. Why, then, if ceramics were so abundant in ancient times, would anyone have wanted to repair a pot? One reason might have been a scarcity of pottery in a particular area. Another, very probably, was that as pottery became more of an art form and the techniques and methods of production became more skilful – as, for example, with Greek vases – the increased expense of replacing certain items would have made it worthwhile to repair them, or at least to prevent cracks from spreading. In ancient China the earliest porcelain was made for the Emperor's court; later, in Europe, factories were opened under the patronage of royalty. Fine china, therefore, was something that most lesser mortals could not afford to possess. In these circumstances, a lower official would be pleased to repair a broken or discarded vessel, which he could then call his own. The beautiful technique known as the 'gold repair' (*see p. 23*) is surely an indication that fine porcelain was as highly valued as gold itself.

ABOVE A highly decorated neck amphora, an ancient Greek wine vessel, dating from approximately 520 BC.

RIGHT Pottery platters being excavated on a site at Tell es-Sa'idiyeh, in Jordan.

LEFT Post-excavation work at the British Museum: hundreds of pottery sherds being sorted and reconstructed.

The use of adhesives

One of the earliest repair materials we know of is bitumen – a hard, black, brittle substance. It was used as a consolidant to repair leaking vessels, as a filler for small holes and also as an adhesive. Examples of such repairs can be found on objects in the British Museum dating from 5000 BC onwards. Wax was also widely used as an early adhesive on Egyptian ceramics.

ABOVE Bitumen was used to seal the crack on this first-millennium AD Nazca vessel from Peru.

Among the very earliest adhesives, most of which were probably developed for use on materials other than pottery, animal glue was very common. The term 'animal glue' is used to cover a number of different glues all made from the whole or part of an animal, such as fish glue, bone glue, skin glue and so on. Animal glue was used extensively by restorers in the nineteenth century as both an adhesive and a filler; in the latter capacity it was mixed with whiting to form a paste. It was also sold under various trade names in the early twentieth century; Pearl Glue® and Seccotine® are both basically animal glues.

Wheat grain or wheat flour, either boiled or steamed, were much-used early adhesives, probably because they were so widely available. Several wheat-based recipes survive, mostly including additives such as lime, isinglass or vinegar. Examples can be found in a late seventeenth-century manuscript, *Mo Ê Hsiao Lu*. This and all the other Chinese recipes quoted in this chapter are mentioned in *Ching-tê-Chên T'ao Lu* (An Account of Ching-tê-Chên Pottery), translated in 1951 by Geoffrey Sayer in *The Potteries of China*:

> *Take some gluten of wheat that has not yet been fully steamed [and] add a little finely sifted lime. Pound it several hundred times and it will suddenly turn as it were to water. Use this as a paste and bind firmly. Dry off in the shade, and it will not come apart but will hold better than rivets. You must not, however, leave water to stand in the vessel for a long period. Again, for every kind of crack and break in any porcelain vessel use glutinous rice congee mixed with white of egg, beat it into a very sticky glue, then add a little powder [the writer does not state what powder this is] and beat it again. Used for sticking damaged parts of porcelain this is also reliable.*

Further on, the manuscript advises the use of egg white and lime together, this time combined with bamboo resin:

> *To stick together pieces of Kuan ware take some white of egg and mix it uniformly with lime; then take the white and put it on one side; then take green bamboo, and collect its resin by burning; then blend the white of egg and the bamboo resin in equal proportions and boil it up into a paste. Stick the paste on to the broken parts of the Kuan ware, and bind it tightly with string; put it into water for a minute or two; place it for three to five days in a shady place; and then take off the binding string. Its firm grip is remarkable. Moreover there are no signs of the damage.*

A second late seventeenth-century manuscript, *Yün Ku Wo Yü*, states:

> *If a piece of Ting ware gets cracked one can use mulberry tree juice, pasting it thickly on the crack and binding it round very tightly. After it has dried in a shady place it will never come apart.*

Mrs Beeton's book on household management when first published in 1861 contained, along with much other advice for the housemaid, this recipe for a china-mending cement:

> *A neat-handed housemaid may sometimes repair these breakages, where they are not broken in very conspicuous places, by joining the pieces very neatly together with a cement made as follows:– Dissolve an ounce of gum mastic in a quantity of highly-rectified spirits of wine; then soften an ounce of isinglass in warm water, and, finally, dissolve it in rum or brandy, till it forms a thick jelly. Mix the isinglass and gum mastic together, adding a quarter of an ounce of finely-powdered gum ammoniac; put the whole into an earthen pipkin, and in a warm place, till they are thoroughly incorporated together; pour it into a small phial, and cork it down for use.*
>
> *In using it, dissolve a small piece of the cement in a silver teaspoon over a lighted candle. The broken piece of glass or china being warmed, and touched with the now liquid cement, join the parts neatly together and hold*

in their places till the cement has set; then wipe away the cement adhering to the edge of the join, and leave it for twelve hours without touching it: the joint will be as strong as the china itself, and if neatly done it will show no joining. It is essential that neither of the pieces be wetted either with hot or cold water.

It was not until the 1915 edition that Mrs Beeton's recipe was changed:
Powdered quick lime mixed with white of egg and a whey of milk and vinegar in equal parts, the whole beaten well and slightly warmed, makes an excellent cement for mending broken china. Wares of all kinds, from the coarsest kitchen utensils to fine porcelain, can also be repaired by the same means.

Some twelve years after Mrs Beeton's first recipe appeared, Ernest Spon published his *Workshop Receipts* in which he described a number of cements and their uses. The recipe for Armenian or Jewellers' Cement in this book is exactly the same as that advised for use on china in the 1861 edition of Mrs Beeton. The adhesives recommended for ceramics are:
London Cement – Boil a piece of Gloucester cheese three times in water, each time allowing the water to evaporate. Take the paste thus left and thoroughly incorporate with dry quick-lime. It will mend glass, wood, china &c., very effectually.
Chinese Cement – Finest pale orange shellac, broken small, 4oz.; rectified spirit (the strongest 58 o.p.) 3oz.; disgest (sic) together in a corked bottle in a warm place until dissolved; it should have the consistence of treacle. For wood, glass, ivory, jewellery and all fancy works, used.

Spon also gives some advice for using cement:
Take as small a quantity of the cement as possible, and bring the cement itself into intimate contact with the surfaces to be united. If glue is employed, the surface should be made so warm that the melted glue is not chilled before it has time to effect a thorough adhesion. Cements that are used in a fused state, as resin or shellac, will not adhere unless the parts to be joined are heated to the fusing point of cement. . . . but if the cement is applied to them while they are cold it will not stick at all. This fact is well known to the itinerant vendors of cement for uniting earthenware. By heating two pieces of china or earthenware so that they will fuse shellac, they are able to smear them with a little of this gum, and join the pieces so that they will rather break at any other part than along the line of union. But although people constantly see the operation performed, and buy liberally of the cement, it will be found nine cases out of ten that the cement proves worthless in the hands of the purchasers, simply because they do not know how to use it. They are afraid to heat a delicate glass or porcelain vessel to a

sufficient degree, or they are apt to use too much of the material, and
the result is failure.

Shellac, the secretion of an insect of the *Coccidae* family, was in common use in the Middle and the Far East, Africa and Europe from the seventeenth century onwards, and doubtless owed its popularity to its water-resistant properties. It is the adhesive most frequently encountered by restorers dismantling old repairs and is the most troublesome to deal with because of its tendency to stain (*see p. 31*); it can also be extremely difficult if not impossible to remove if it has cross-linked, or chemically bonded.

The twentieth century saw the introduction of commercially mass-produced adhesives such as Seccotine® (animal glue), Durofix® (cellulose nitrate) and, later, epoxy resins such as Araldite®. After thirty years as a restorer I can confirm that 'if it's sticky, someone will have used it to repair ceramics at some time', adding the rider that it doesn't always even have to be sticky!

The use of metal clamps

Riveting

It is not clear when the riveting of porcelain began, although we do know that this method of repair was in general use in seventeenth-century China. A further clue can be found in the sixteenth-century manuscript *Shih Ch'ing Jih Cha*:

> *As for cracked pieces one hears that on the Tiger Hill in Su-chou there are people capable of repairing them. This is called 'Tight binding'.*

Most of the riveted objects we encounter nowadays, however, were repaired during the Victorian era. Some display quite ingenious and decorative ways of holding the pieces together (*see opposite, above*). In one case that I came across, the rivets on a plate had been skilfully sculpted so that they looked like three small, metal cats crouching on the surface.

There are, in fact, a few people who still employ the technique, and some readers may consider it inappropriate to place riveting in this historical section, since to class it as an 'old method' might be thought an insult to those who still use it. Most modern restorers, however, consider it unnecessary, ugly, destructive – since it is likely to cause chipping (*opposite, bottom right*) – and potentially corrosive – since some types of metal rivet may stain porcelain (*opposite, bottom left*). I personally dislike riveting but can understand, though I am not entirely convinced by, the arguments put forward by those restorers who point out that domestic china repaired with synthetic resins and used every day is subject to weakening by both hot and cold water, detergents and grease, whereas rivets are not affected by any of these factors. There are five main stages in riveting:

1 Marking the rivet position
2 Drilling the holes
3 Washing the china
4 Pulling the rivets
5 Filling the holes

The first two rivets are positioned one at either end of the join or crack, with the remainder placed about 4cm (1½in) apart, following the line of the break. Small marks are made on the porcelain where the rivet holes are to be drilled, and from each a line is drawn at right angles to the fracture. This is most important, for the angle of the clamp must be correct in order to exert the right amount of pressure on the break. The hole for the rivet is then drilled, not necessarily all the way through depending on the thickness of the china, using a hand-operated string drill with a diamond tip. Alternatively, a small electric drill, such as the type employed by jewellers, could be used. Either type of drill allows the control needed over the operation while leaving one hand free to hold the china. The holes are drilled at an angle of 15–20° towards the fracture. This prevents the rivets from coming out, as they would do if the holes were vertically drilled. The china is then washed with detergents or chemicals according to the preference of the restorer.

Making a rivet involves cutting a piece of wire with a D-shaped section to a length approximately twice that of the distance between the holes. One end of

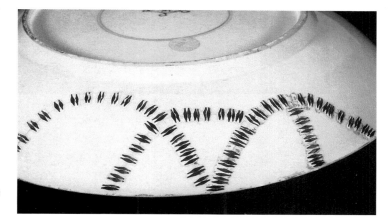

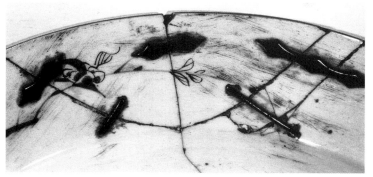

TOP Decorative brass rivets on the back of a large *famille verte* seventeenth-century dish.

ABOVE Finely cut and decorative rivets on the back of a Chinese plate.

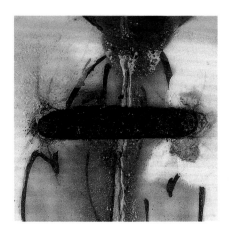

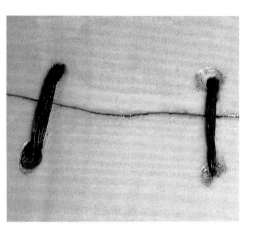

FAR LEFT Detail of an oriental-style dish showing the staining that is typically caused when an iron rivet corrodes.

LEFT Rivets made from wire filaments. The chips made by the drill can be clearly seen.

the wire is held in a pair of flat-nosed pliers and bent to match the angle of the prepared hole. Any excess wire on the newly formed leg is cut off and the end filed flat. The half-made rivet is then placed in the appropriate hole – it should not be visible on the other face of the object. The distance between the holes is carefully measured and marked on the rivet, which is then removed and bent a fraction short of the required length, so that when it is in place it will be under slight tension. The second leg is cut to the same length as the first, and the end filed flat, as before.

In the next stage, the rivet is refitted into position and pulled with the pliers until the other end slips neatly into its hole. If it has been fitted correctly, the rivet should lie flat along the face of the china (*see p. 17*). Finally the holes are filled with plaster of Paris, which is then smoothed down. In some rare cases, the rivets are coloured to match the china; usually, however, they are left unpainted.

The process may be taken a step further by sinking the rivets into the china so that they finish flush with the surface. This effect is achieved by cutting a channel between the drilled holes into which the rivet fits.

Sometimes rivets are bound with wire to give them extra strength. This method is mainly used on spouts or handles, and involves winding tinned copper or lead wire around the rivet – in much the same way as you might bind the handle of a cricket bat.

The above description may make riveting sound easy – in fact, it demands a high degree of skill. Few of the riveted pieces that I have seen have been entirely successful. It is not unusual to come across objects that have been riveted on both faces – an unnecessary precaution if the job is done correctly. Again, it is not unusual to see ill-fitting rivets standing proud of the surface of the china, with plaster of Paris pushed under them to correct the fault and prevent movement along the line of the fracture.

Tying and lacing

Two other methods of repair using metal clamps are known as 'tying' and 'lacing'. The terms are self-explanatory. The first method involves tying metal wire around the fracture and then soldering the ends to prevent them from coming apart. This procedure may be used on, for example, a plate with an open latticework rim. Lacing is a more elaborate form of tying, in which holes are drilled in the porcelain on either side of the break and wire is laced through; the ends are then twisted and soldered together.

Dowelling

Dowelling of porcelain figures (*see opposite*) and handles was a common practice during the Victorian period, and some restorers still use this method today. It consists of drilling a hole in each of the fragments to be joined and fixing the dowel, made of wood or metal, into one of the holes with an adhesive

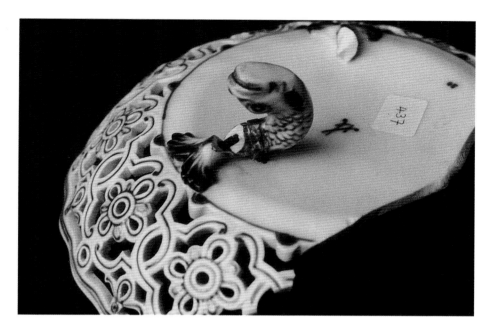

LEFT An iron dowel and metal band used to secure the foot on an early eighteenth-century Meissen pierced-work bowl. (Private collection)

or a filling material. The first hole is drilled slightly larger than the dowel and the second as large as the fragment permits, so as to allow for any possible misalignment of the fragments. Adhesive is applied all over the dowel and along the fractured edge. The two halves are then pushed together so that the dowel is concealed inside the porcelain. With porcelain figures, which are usually cast and therefore mainly hollow, the adhesive is packed into the cavity and the dowel pushed into the adhesive while it is still soft. Some metals, however, are liable to corrode and thus stain the object (*see pp. 46–7*), and any dowel may expand in adverse conditions, causing cracking and, in some cases, the complete break-up of the porcelain.

Restoration

Joining pieces of porcelain is, in many cases, not the only repair necessary; missing fragments often have to be replaced as well. This operation has been effected in a variety of ways in the past. The earliest manuscript to record a method of restoring ceramics is the sixteenth-century *Shih Ch'ing Jih Cha*, which advises refiring:

> If old pieces of porcelain from any famous kiln such as censers lack ears or feet or if vases have damaged mouth-rims, one can use old bits to patch the old (sic); and if one adds glaze and then bakes it it is just the same as the old. But the colour is weak at the patch. Yet people prefer this to new stuff. And if one uses the method of blowing the glaze on to the patched part there is still less of a trace.

RIGHT A nineteenth-century insert in a sixteenth-century Iznic dish. The join line of the recent restoration has been left undecorated so that the historic repair can be seen.

This type of restoration – where a missing fragment is replaced and a glaze is painted, dipped or blown on – has been practised almost as long as porcelain has been produced, and in some cases was carried out by the original potters when a glaze was found to be faulty at the time of manufacture. Early restorers composed their own glazes, which could be fired at a lower temperature than the original, and for a final finish they dipped the whole article into the new glaze and then refired it. Although the ethics of the technique may be questioned, there is no doubt that the results are often visually very satisfactory.

From earliest times, restorers have used fragments from other ceramic objects to replace missing portions of the pieces under repair. I once had to deal with a plate that had been restored in the bazaar in Istanbul between 1900 and 1910, as I was informed by the owner. A piece from a completely different plate had been used to fill the gap. The edge of the fracture had been filed smooth and the new piece cut to size and stuck in with shellac. The surface of the inserted piece had then been extensively overpainted in oils to imitate the pattern of the repaired plate. A similar type of repair was found on a sixteenth-century Iznic dish from the Godman collection in the British Museum (*see above*). The colours and decoration matched so well that the replacement piece could have come from a contemporary dish; in this case, however, as scientific analysis revealed, the new piece dated from the late nineteenth century and had been made especially to fill the gap. In another example, the latticework on a bowl had been repaired using the lattice from another bowl: the pieces matched so well that it was difficult to distinguish the join. This repair may have been done by the potter or, more likely, by someone with access to the factory wasters. In some extreme cases, two different halves were joined to form a complete piece.

Filing of edges to make pieces fit was very common practice and was usually done when an assembly was not correct, thus smoothing and concealing the evidence of a poor repair. By contrast, it is also possible to find examples where large steps, like castellations, have been cut into the edges to help the bonding process.

All the major English factories had their own restorers, to whom they sent their damaged pieces; evidence of this practice can be found in records of payment to restorers in the company accounts. Receipts from the Bow and Chelsea factories show that during the latter part of the eighteenth century there were several restorers working in St Martin's Lane, London, possibly as a small community to which the big factories could bring their wasters to be corrected. The same system had been used earlier in China, according to one of the old manuscripts, which refers to 'neat-handed people' who lived outside the village factories and could repair any faults that occurred during firing.

Occasionally unfired clay was used as a filler, although it must have been difficult to achieve a good fit with this material because of the shrinkage factor. When dry, it must have been quite fragile – sometimes it was fired before insertion to make it harder (although in these cases allowance would have had to be made for further shrinkage). The most common gap-filler, however, was plaster of Paris, sometimes with additives, such as alum, to harden it.

In some cases metal was used as a base for some other kind of finish, such as plaster of Paris. The metal – usually lead because of its malleability – was shaped and fitted by dowelling, riveting or

BELOW Replacement metal handle, lid and spout on a Ming dynasty Chinese ewer (c.1522–66).

RIGHT Detail of a Chinese Qing dynasty porcelain teapot (*c.*1770–80) showing a basket-weave handle made of cane, attached by means of metal dowels and facings.

lacing, and then covered with the liquid plaster, which, when dry, was smoothed to give the desired finish.

Metal was more commonly used in the replacement of handles, which were fixed by drilling holes in the porcelain, pushing the metal through the holes and burring it over to prevent the handles from coming out (*see p. 21*). Any remains of the original handles were usually ground away first. In another example, an iron cage-work, incorporating handles, was built around the body of a jug and soldered together. Corrosion of these metal inserts is a problem, as they stain both the glaze and body of the object. Although metal was the most popular choice for replacing handles and so on, other materials were sometimes used (*see left*).

Colouring

Inserted fragments are usually, though not always, coloured to match the repaired object. In the past, oil paints were the colouring medium most commonly used; when first applied they are almost shiny enough to make false glazing unnecessary. Water paints were sometimes used because of their fine texture, though it would have been necessary to stabilize them with a false glaze. In my early days as a porcelain restorer I used powder colour mixed with shellac, thinned if necessary with a little industrial methylated spirit. (Shellac and powder pigments can still be used for earthenware and stoneware.) With all these different painting methods, yellowing – particularly of white – occurs within a short period of time.

Oriental restorers devised an ingenious and beautiful way of restoring damaged porcelain – the method known as the 'gold repair' (*see opposite*). The object was stuck together and filled with Japanese or Chinese lacquer and a layer of gold leaf was then applied to the restored area and burnished. The

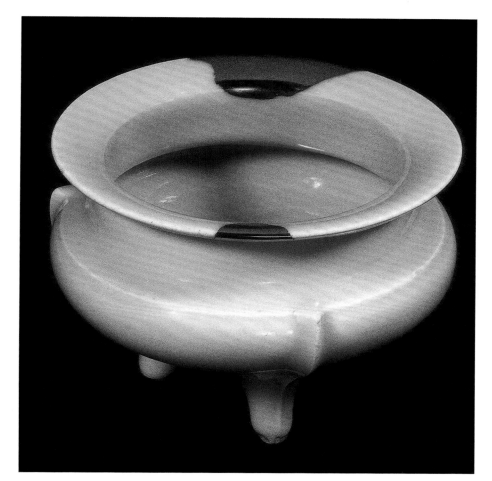

LEFT An ancient gold repair to the rim of a Song dynasty celadon incense burner.

technique not only avoided the difficulty of precise colour matching and the problem of discoloration, but when skilfully done, as it invariably was, actually enhanced the beauty and value of the object. Some gold repairs to Japanese ceramics are known to have been carried out as early as the sixteenth century.

In this chapter I have outlined the more commonly found methods that have been used in the past, but they are certainly not the only ones – some very strange and eccentric restorations and recipes can turn up. One book, for example, recommends as an adhesive that old school favourite, tapioca pudding, and I once saw a porcelain cup and a Delft plate that had both been stuck with fine Portland cement. On another occasion I found, on dismantling an old repair to an Islamic long-necked vase, that its neck had been restored by using the metal end of an electric light bulb as a sleeve to join the two halves together. When dealing with old restorations, be prepared for anything!

2 Documentation and examination

When a piece of porcelain first arrives in your workroom there are certain preliminaries to be carried out before the process of repair actually begins. These steps can be summarized as:

• Documentation, including record photography.
• Examination, to determine composition, present damage, possible previous repairs and the best method of restoration.

Documenting the object

Before starting any work on a piece of porcelain it is necessary to enter the object into the workroom records. These should contain all the basic information you will need to know, such as:

1 The date the object was brought into the workroom.
2 The workroom number assigned to the object.
3 A simple description of the object – for example, 'a blue and white bowl with floral decoration, diameter at rim 30cm (12in), height 17.5cm (7in); thought to be Chinese fifteenth century'.
4 The name, address and telephone number of the owner.
5 The name of the person who received the object.
6 A detailed account of what is wrong with the object and what the owner would like done in terms of repair or restoration, as well as a note of the lighting conditions, if known, under which the object will be kept or displayed (you will need to bear this last piece of information in mind when you come to colour match any restored areas).
7 An estimate of the time the work could take. (You may also want to record the time it actually took.)
8 An itemized estimate of the cost, including labour.
9 The signature of the owner confirming acceptance of the estimate.
10 The date by which the object is required, or that by which you have promised to have it ready. (Agreement on this should, if possible, be delayed until you have completed a full examination.)

Keep a separate file for any correspondence between you and the owner. It is in your interest to obtain the owner's written acceptance of your estimate before starting work on the object. It is also advisable to discuss the question of insurance with the owner before receiving the object, to establish where the responsibility lies should any accident happen while it is in your care.

The object should then be photographed with its workroom number displayed clearly on a card somewhere within the picture area. The type of camera with a 'data back' – a special feature that records the date on each frame of film – would be useful but is by no means essential. Further information about the object may be added later, as it becomes available:

LEFT Using a binocular microscope to examine the detail on a porcelain figure.

1 The name(s) of the restorer(s) who will do the work, or any part of it.
2 A record of any photographs that are taken.
3 Detailed notes on the composition and colour of the body, pattern, glaze and gilding seen during the examination of the broken edges of the object prior to restoration work commencing.
4 A detailed account of the restoration carried out and the materials used.
5 The date the object was returned to the owner with his/her signature, or that of a representative, as proof of receipt.

Examining the object

The first thing you need to establish is the type of body you are dealing with: for example, hard-paste porcelain, soft-paste porcelain, bone china or glazed white earthenware. It is often extremely difficult to distinguish between some of these types – some white earthenwares could easily be mistaken for soft-paste porcelain – though it may be of help to know that a particular factory produced hard- or soft-paste porcelain or that, at a certain date, there was a change in the type of paste used. There are ways of telling hard- and soft-paste porcelain apart, however (*see box, right*).

Hard- and soft-paste porcelain
Hard-paste porcelain and bone china are usually much whiter in colour than soft-paste or white earthenware, but bone china is not as highly fired as hard-paste. The broken edge of hard-paste porcelain is smooth whereas that of soft-paste and white earthenware is much more grainy. If you are still not sure, you can place a small drop of water on to a broken edge. If it is not absorbed, the body is probably hard-paste; quick absorption indicates that you are dealing with earthenware, with other types of body somewhere in between.

RIGHT Discoloration can be clearly seen on the restored and painted hand of this seventeenth- to eighteenth-century Chinese Buddha from the Qing dynasty.

RIGHT Discoloration can be clearly seen on the restored and painted hand of this seventeenth- to eighteenth-century Chinese Buddha from the Qing dynasty.

There are certain features to look for from the outset, because they are the ones that are likely to cause you the most trouble. It is important, for example, to examine the surface decoration of the piece: is gilding present and, if so, what is its condition? If areas are missing then it is probably a soft, low-fired gilding that could be easily damaged, and so you will need to take particular care when working on the object. The same goes for other overglaze decorations, such as enamels or transfers.

If there are stains, typically near a crack or chip, a treatment that involves soaking can cause them to spread further into the body of the object, thus exacerbating the already difficult problem of removing them.

Most of the examination will be done simply by looking at the object and seeing what is wrong with it, but sound and touch also play a part. If there is a crack, for example, vessels will rattle or sound dull when tapped with your knuckle, rather than responding with a clear ringing sound. Repairs will often feel rough or warm, or both. You will be unlikely to miss an old repair anyway, because it will probably be very discoloured (*see opposite*), though it may be more difficult to ascertain the extent of that repair and the material that was used to make it.

The first chapter of the book will at least have given you some idea of the many different types of adhesives that have been used in the past. In looking for *recent* repairs you can be caught out very easily, as some modern restorers are so skilled at covering their tracks that even an expert can be deceived (*see pp. 28 and 29*). This task becomes less daunting with experience. The more restorations you have done, the easier it is to pinpoint flaws in other people's work, as they are likely to be the same kinds of flaw as those you have noticed in your own work. The most common faults to look out for are:

- A build-up of paint on the surface.
- 'Misting' at the edges of sprayed areas.
- 'Steps' where fragments have not been perfectly joined.
- Sagging of paint layers.
- Small holes in filled areas.
- Absence, change in colour or grainy appearance of gilding.
- Signs of restoration on the inside of a piece – the area where the restorer sometimes gets careless.

Glaze and decoration

Once you have established the composition and present condition of a piece, and the extent and nature of previous repairs, if any, you have then to decide what needs to be done and the best way of seeing the work through. Your chosen course of action will depend partly on experience but after reading this book you will, I hope, have a much better idea of how to proceed. There are two very important points that you must always consider: first, the strength and colour of the glaze and the body and, second, at which stage in the manufacture the decoration was applied.

It is vital that you find out the hardness of the glaze, as this will affect your choice of filler and determine which cutting tools and abrasive papers you can safely use on the piece. I am not suggesting that a very hard glaze will resist damage if you sand over it while smoothing down the fill: there is always a danger that your tools will mark the original glaze. Over the years, I have seen

RIGHT Viewed in ordinary light, the repair to this European bowl, decorated in oriental style, is invisible (*see opposite*). (Private collection)

far too many beautiful pieces badly scratched in this way, or with large areas over-sprayed in order to hide such blemishes. If you are not certain of the strength of the glaze, turn the object over and perform a hardness test on a small, inconspicuous area of the base. Any abrasive paper, file or cutting tool that scratches the surface is too harsh. If the glaze is very soft, you may have to think about using a softer filler.

By examining any broken edges with a small magnifying glass you can learn much about how the object was manufactured. You should carry out this type of examination in daylight if possible – bright, indirect light is best. Do not trust artificial light, as it tends to impart a blue or yellow colour. Look carefully at the colour of the body – is it truly white, as it appears to the naked eye, or has it a bluish or brownish tinge? Study the glaze and decoration in the same way; you should be able to detect in section on the broken edges three (or four) layers, for example: body, pattern then glaze; body, glaze then pattern; or either of these combinations and then gilding. The higher the temperature at which the object has been fired, though, the more the glaze and pattern will have fused together and the harder it will be to distinguish between the layers. You should try to determine whether the decoration was applied under or over the glaze before firing or whether it was applied after the glaze firing. If it is underglaze, there is often some bleeding of the colour into the body, whereas an overglaze colour is more likely to be suspended in the glaze layer. 'On glaze' enamels are applied after firing and the object is then refired at a lower temperature to fuse them to the glaze; they are easy to distinguish from underglaze or overglaze decoration because they sit slightly proud of the surface. These factors will determine how you apply your decorative restoration, so it is important to take careful notes at this stage.

Equipment

There are two pieces of equipment that will be of help to you when you are examining a piece of porcelain. They are expensive and you can manage without them, but they do allow a much closer scrutiny of the object, which may reveal restoration previously unsuspected if the work has been very skilfully done.

The first piece of equipment is a good binocular microscope, and the second is an ultraviolet lamp. You will find that under ultraviolet (UV) illumination restored areas often fluoresce with a white light, while the original porcelain takes on a dark violet colour (*see above*). The UV light must be used in total darkness and it works by showing the difference in absorbency between the original porcelain and the synthetic material used in the restoration. Bear in mind, however, that areas which fluoresce white may not necessarily be total restoration; they could just be layers of paint that have been applied over the original porcelain.

You must use an ultraviolet lamp with care, making sure that your skin and eyes are not exposed to its rays. Always wear cotton gloves and special goggles when using this type of illumination.

3 Dismantling and cleaning

Now that you have completed your minute scrutiny of the object and taken detailed notes and photographs, you are ready to start work on the first stage of the restoration process. If there is no previous repair or restoration present, you will be able to dispense with the next section, but you will still need to carry out a thorough cleaning process (*see pp. 41–7*) before proceeding to the next chapter.

Dismantling

When you are presented with an object that has previously been restored, it can sometimes be difficult to decide whether it should be dismantled or not. If the previous repair is old, loose, discoloured or generally disfiguring, the decision is obvious. If, however, the object has been recently restored, then the choice may not be quite so straightforward, especially if the restoration is, to all appearances, satisfactory. Some restorers use a technique that might be termed 'partial dismantling'. I cannot recommend this process. Using a strong solvent to dismantle any part of a piece can be dangerous, as the very fumes could weaken those joins that the restorer has no intention of dismantling, with the possibility that they could give way at any time in the future.

So my advice is either dismantle completely, or not at all – although you must bear in mind that if you decide not to dismantle apparently sound joins, you are running a risk. Unless you can analyse the adhesive, you will probably have little idea of what was used to mend the break; even if you can identify it you may not be able to tell whether or not it was mixed to the correct consistency. There is always a danger that the joins may give way at any stage of the restoration process that you yourself carry out. This risk can be reduced, however, if you consolidate the joins by applying with a pipette an appropriate adhesive thinned with a solvent.

Preliminary stages

Once you have decided that a repaired object must be taken apart, the next task is to determine whether you will have to take any special steps before starting.

If the object is gilded or has any other delicate overglaze decoration you will need to make a test on some inconspicuous area to ensure that even gentle solvents are safe to use. If the restored areas have been painted, the paint layer must first be removed in order to expose the adhesive used in the old repair and to make it easier to identify. Test the paint carefully with the flat edge of a surgical scalpel to see if it will flake off easily. If it does not, you will need to use a solvent to soften it. It is advisable to try alcohols, acetone or white spirit before turning to stronger agents, such as paint stripper. Soak white tissue paper in your chosen solvent and apply it to the area, covering it with aluminium foil to slow down evaporation. Once the paint has softened, you can easily remove it with a tissue or a spatula.

With the join lines now revealed, it may be possible to identify by colour and texture the adhesive that has been used for the original restoration. Colour alone can be misleading, though, as some adhesives discolour to almost identical shades. If you are in any doubt, you will need to remove a small piece and test it with various solvents.

Adhesives

The following list will help you to identify a range of adhesives by indicating the colour they should be, how hard they should be and, most importantly, the best solvents to use to soften them.

Animal glue (bone, skin or fish)

This is a widely used adhesive, sometimes with the addition of whiting.
How to identify: Normally transparent to pale yellow in colour but it can occasionally be brown. Soft (in comparison with other adhesives) when tested with a scalpel.
Best solvents to use: Warm water, steam. Animal glue breaks down extremely quickly and is easy to remove.

Shellac

This, the most widely employed of all the old adhesives, was first used in China.
How to identify: Orange/very dark brown in colour. Very hard and brittle, and the older the shellac, the more brittle it will be. It is very difficult to break down with commercially available products. If naturally occurring dyes were not removed during the original processing of this organic resin, there may well be staining, which is usually pink in colour. Black staining may indicate shellac that has been burned during application.
Best solvent to use: Industrial methylated spirit (IMS).

Epoxy resin

This type of resin may have been used as early as 1930, but its presence usually indicates a post-war repair. It is the most widely used adhesive in modern porcelain repairs.
How to identify: It ranges from a light yellow/green to a dark yellow/dark brown colour, depending on its age. All epoxies eventually yellow to some degree, although some of the newest water-white resins take much longer to do so. Epoxy is generally very hard, but not brittle. If it has been badly mixed you may be able to mark it with your fingernail. It is often hard to distinguish from rubber adhesives by sight alone.
Best solvents to use: Solvents cause epoxy to swell and soften rather than

dissolve. Start with warm to hot water or acetone, though these will work only if the epoxy has been badly mixed. If they have no effect, try Nitromors®, Polystrippa® or dichloromethane – even pineapple juice (yes, it does work because of the enzymes, but you will have to wait longer for a result and the object comes out very sticky). Even if the epoxy does not break down after repeated applications of paint stripper, it will certainly have been weakened, and immersion of the object in warm to hot water may then do the trick.

Rubber adhesives

How to identify: These are very similar in their colour to epoxy resin – hence the potential confusion. If you can extract a small sample from the join, take it between your fingernails and pull. If it stretches, it is rubber; if it breaks, it is more likely to be an epoxy resin.
Best solvents to use: Nitromors® or Polystrippa®. Some types of rubber adhesive may soften in warm water, allowing you to pull the join apart.

Polyvinyl acetate (PVA); Polyvinyl alcohol (PVOH)

How to identify: These substances range from clear/white to soft yellow when new, but age to a deeper yellow. They have a similar appearance to rubber adhesives, but are easy to identify because they turn white when placed in water. They form a skin that can be very difficult to remove, especially from soft-bodied objects.
Best solvents to use: Warm water, acetone, white spirit or Nitromors®.

Polyester

How to identify: It ranges from light to dark yellow. It has a tendency to cross-link with age and is hard, though not brittle. Polyester can be difficult to remove, as solvents tend to soften rather than dissolve it.
Best solvents to use: Nitromors®, Polystrippa® or dichloromethane.

Cellulose nitrate

How to identify: In general it is water-white, though it acquires a yellow tinge with age. The early form of this adhesive is liable to become brittle after long periods. Modern brands contain a plasticizer that makes them more stable.
Best solvents to use: Acetone or IMS.

Cyanoacrylate

How to identify: This is a relatively new adhesive, clear when new and ageing to light yellow. It tends to be brittle.
Best solvents to use: Acetone, Nitromors® or Polystrippa®.

Sometimes it will prove difficult, if not impossible, to identify the original adhesive, particularly in the case of early resins. If you are unsure, start with the

Warning
When using solvents other than water, always follow health and safety regulations. Whenever possible, use a fume cupboard if you are working with large quantities of solvent or whenever you open saturated-atmosphere containers; otherwise always wear appropriate safety clothing – mask, gloves and goggles.

weakest solvent, water, and work your way through to the strongest. It is wise to follow this procedure for the sake of both your health and your pocket: water is cheap and in plentiful supply; paint stripper is relatively expensive and contains chemicals that can be dangerous if the appropriate health and safety procedures are not followed.

Solvents and dismantling methods

In recent times there has been a move away from immersing objects in solvents and towards dismantling by saturated atmosphere. There is a good reason for this: an object that has been immersed in a solution of solvent or water will take much longer to dry out than one that has been dismantled in a saturated atmosphere. The time a ceramic body takes to dry out is dependent on its size, its composition, the temperature of the room and whether a volatile solvent or water was used. It is essential that the body of the object be allowed to dry completely before sticking because any trapped moisture could adversely affect the properties of the adhesive. Where you have no option other than deep soaking because the object will not come apart any other way, make certain to allow adequate drying time before proceeding to the next stage.

Whichever solvent or method you choose, the time taken to dismantle the object will depend on the type and strength of the adhesive that has been used in the original repair.

Water

Soaking

First, find a plastic container of a suitable size. Line the bottom with a flat piece of foam rubber or similar material, to protect any fragments of porcelain that may fall as the adhesive breaks down. Place the object on the foam rubber and fill the container with hand-hot water. Never use boiling water, as it might cause the porcelain to crack and overglaze enamels to spring off. As a general rule, the finer the porcelain the cooler the water should be.

Leave the object submerged in the water for at least two hours, or longer if the porcelain is very thick. If after this time the joins have not come apart, apply a little pressure to them before removing the object from the water. It is always possible that the adhesive has softened sufficiently for you to dismantle the piece, and it is far better for it to collapse while in the container than when you are carrying it across the workroom. A word of caution: if there are any (either organic or inorganic) stains present – more likely with soft-paste porcelain – prolonged soaking in water is not recommended, as this is likely to cause the stains to spread and disfigure the object (*see pp. 46–7*).

Saturated atmosphere

Unless you are dealing with an adhesive that is likely to break down quickly, such as animal glue, this method is not ideal. Water needs to be kept boiling if

Drying times compared

In an experiment, two previously dismantled objects – a saucer of hard-paste and a teacup of soft-paste porcelain – were weighed before being submerged in water and left for three hours. They were removed, wiped dry, then weighed again immediately and subsequently each day until they had returned to their original weight. In temperatures of about 23°C (73°F), the hard-paste saucer took two days and the soft-paste cup four days to dry out completely. (Earthenware takes a great deal longer because it is so porous.)

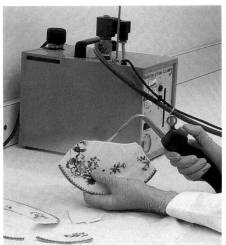

you are to maintain a steamy atmosphere; once the water starts to cool it becomes less effective. Place the object in the most airtight container you have available, supporting it with a suitable material, and add a bowl of boiling water. Seal the container immediately and check every fifteen minutes or so to see if the joins have come apart. If not, renew the boiling water and continue checking until the adhesive has broken down – or you decide to try a different solvent. If the object is too large to fit into a container, you can use a black bin liner or a garden waste bag.

Steam

One piece of equipment recently adopted to dismantle water-soluble adhesives is the steam cleaner (*see above right*). Use it as described on page 46, directing the nozzle along the line of the break. Dismantle the object piece by piece, starting at the top and working down.

Acetone

Acetone is the least effective of the solvents when used on fully cured adhesives, but it is quite successful at softening newly mixed resin. It should always be kept away from any source of heat, as it is very flammable. A glass vessel, preferably a desiccator (*see above left*), is ideal for the purpose; polythene is a possible alternative but plastic could be dissolved by the acetone. Always keep the container covered because acetone is extremely volatile.

Soaking

This is not the best way to use acetone, unless the object is very small, as the acetone evaporates extremely quickly, probably before it has had a chance to do its work (although covering the container may help a little), and the large amounts that would probably be needed would present a considerable fire risk.

Put the object in a glass container, cushioned on a few layers of tissue if necessary, cover it with acetone and seal the container to prevent evaporation.

Saturated atmosphere

Cushion the object on wads of tissue in an airtight container or a polythene bag, together with some acetone in an open glass vessel (something like a saucer or a flat dish is preferable, as it will speed up the evaporation process). As a solvent, acetone works extremely quickly, if it is going to work at all, so leave it in the container for only a few hours.

Swab method

This is a useful technique if there is only a single fragment to remove from an otherwise undamaged piece, or if the object is so large that you cannot find a container of sufficient size to accommodate it. Cut strips of cotton wool about 2.5cm (1in) wide and dip them into the acetone using a pair of tweezers. Alternatively, use strips of tissue paper of the same width and at least three layers thick. Place the strips along the line of the break and press them on to the surface so that they make good contact. Then cover the strips with aluminium foil to slow down evaporation. Because acetone is so volatile, you will have to add more of the solvent to the cotton wool or tissue paper every twenty minutes or so. This can be done through a small hole in the foil, without removing it, using either a syringe or an eye-dropper. The length of time acetone takes to break down the joins will depend on the type of adhesive used; it is worth checking after about half an hour, although you may have to wait a lot longer than this. After dismantling the object, be sure to check the broken edges for any fibres of cotton wool and remove them with a stencil brush dipped in acetone or with tweezers.

Industrial methylated spirit (IMS)

Methylated spirit is used to remove shellac. Always use the water-white type if possible rather than the pink type, as this pink colour is a dye that has been known to stain porcelain. IMS can be bought only under licence, but you can use surgical spirit as an alternative, although the process may take longer.

Soaking

IMS is expensive, so you may prefer not to use this method unless the object is very small. (Like other solvents, however, it may be reused for dismantling purposes, if necessary.) Place the object, suitably supported, in a container of IMS, cover it and leave it for a few hours – but check after half an hour.

Saturated atmosphere

This is certainly the most economical way of using IMS. Follow the procedures recommended above for acetone. Seal the container and leave it for one or two days. If the joins have not come apart in that time, continue with the process until they do – or until you decide to try another method or change to a different solvent.

Swab method

Proceed as for acetone. Check every hour until the joins have come apart; on very large objects, the process could take a considerable time – perhaps as long as two or three days. This method can be useful in cases where you want to remove only a single fragment.

Nitromors® and Polystrippa®

These products are commercial paint strippers – Nitromors® is a gel and Polystrippa® a liquid. Both are extremely effective at weakening a whole range of adhesives, including, most importantly, the epoxy resins. There are two different types of Nitromors®: water-soluble, which comes in a green tin; and acetone-soluble, sold in a yellow tin. I always use the water-soluble version because water is nearly always readily available and is much cheaper than acetone. You must always be careful when using any form of paint stripper because it can burn your skin on contact.

Direct application

If the porcelain is soft-paste, it may be prudent to wet the object with water to prevent unnecessary absorption of paint stripper into the body. Apply the stripper along the line of the adhesive, both inside and outside, cover with foil and leave it to penetrate. Unfortunately, paint stripper will dissolve the adhesive that holds paintbrush hairs in place, so use either old brushes or cotton wool buds to apply it. The solvent should be renewed every few hours, as it evaporates very quickly with this method. If you are working on a piece with gilding on it, apply the solvent to the side without the gilding (*see Take care, left*). The adhesive could possibly take a few hours to break down; if it is an epoxy it could take much longer than this – even days or, in some cases, weeks. When the joins have come apart, carefully wash the stripper away with the appropriate solvent (either acetone, if acetone-based, or water, if water-based). Use cold water when washing off paint stripper, as hot water will create noxious fumes (*see Warning, left*).

Saturated atmosphere

This method, which involves placing the object and an open vessel of paint stripper together in an airtight container or (for large objects) a black plastic bag, is not as effective as the direct application method, but it is probably the safest way to dismantle an object that has gilding on it. It would be the preferred method for an object gilded on both sides, or where the gilding appears unstable.

Take care

You must be careful that neither Nitromors® nor Polystrippa® comes into direct contact with any gilded decoration; either of these could damage the gilding beyond repair.

Warning

Clean up any spilled Nitromors® or Polystrippa® on work surfaces at once. Always adhere to the rules governing the use of these solvents. Always use cold water when cleaning up paint stripper; hot water produces a toxic gas.

Dichloromethane

This chemical forms the basis of commercial paint strippers and can be purchased from chemical suppliers. Its advantage lies in the fact that, being much thinner in consistency than commercial strippers, it is easier to use and less messy. However, it is much more expensive and more difficult to obtain.

Saturated atmosphere

The advantage of using dichloromethane for this method is that it is so volatile that the atmosphere inside the airtight container becomes saturated very quickly. Open the container after a few hours to see if the adhesive has begun to soften; if not, reseal it and try again later. This is a very good method for fragile objects and for porcelain decorated with gilding.

Swab method

Follow the procedure used for acetone and IMS. This method could dismantle the object quickly but take care with delicate surface decoration, such as gilding, which could be damaged by the chemical.

Auro® paint-stripping paste; 3M® paint and varnish remover

These two commercial paint strippers appeared on the market comparatively recently. 3M® is an off-white gel and Auro® is caramel coloured and of a much thicker consistency. They are both soluble in water and are useful as less-toxic alternatives to Nitromors® and Polystrippa®, but they do take about three times as long to work. The best method of use would be direct application.

Dismantling fills

Fills normally cause fewer problems than adhesives; not only are they more accessible to work on, but they also often come apart when general dismantling takes place. Plaster of Paris fills, when soaked in warm water, soften enough to be removable from the ceramic; epoxies loosen with the use of Nitromors®. In extreme cases, cut out stubborn fills with the aid of a piercing-saw or a pad-saw. If the fill is surrounded by porcelain, first drill a hole in it, then feed one end of a piercing-saw blade through the hole and reconnect it to the saw. You should now be able to cut out the fill. Remove the small amount left around the edge by loosening it with solvent or, in the case of soft fillers, by breaking it away with a pair of flat-nosed pliers or removing it with a scalpel.

Dismantling metal supports

Restoration that has been carried out with the aid of metal supports, such as riveting or tying and lacing, is easy to see. The same cannot be said, however, about metal dowels, for they will be buried inside the porcelain itself. All metal supports, whether they are visible or not, should be removed if they are causing damage or staining. Iron supports can cause a brown rust stain, bronze a green

stain and lead, on occasion, a grey stain. The description in Chapter 1 of the methods of fitting metal supports should help you to understand how to remove them.

Occasionally, objects in the British Museum that have been riveted, but that show no signs of damage or staining to the ceramic, have had their rivets left *in situ* at the curator's request because of the historical conservation aspect; usually rivets appear on the back of an object and therefore do not usually affect its appearance in a display case.

Rivets

There are two techniques for removing rivets – the 'cut' and the 'pull'. The 'cut' involves cutting the rivets through the middle using a needle file, taking care not to file the glaze. As a precaution, protect the surface on either side of the rivet with masking tape. When the rivet has been cut, you can then pull out the two ends with the aid of a pair of pliers.

The 'pull' method involves passing a thin blade – either a scalpel blade or the hook end of a small spatula – under the rivet, pushing out any plaster packing and levering up one end of the rivet. You can then pull it out with a pair of pliers. This method has two drawbacks: first, it cannot be used on rivets that do not have any packing under them and, second, it increases the risk of chipping off small areas from around the drilled hole.

Common to both methods is the order in which the rivets must be removed. Never start at one end and work towards the other because the last rivets will begin to give way under the strain, allowing the joined edges of the object to

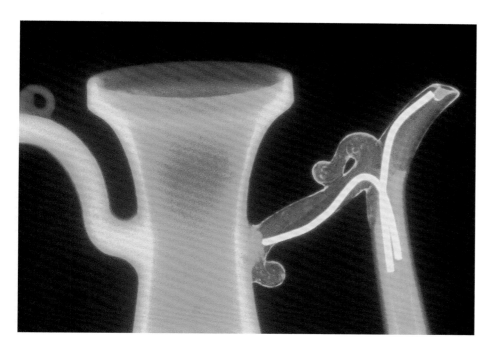

LEFT In this X-ray of the ewer shown opposite, the metal dowels supporting the restoration can be seen clearly.

shift, with the danger that they may grind against each other and flake away areas of glaze along the line of the break. Always remove the middle rivet first and work outwards from it, leaving the two outer rivets until last. Before removing these, it is a good idea to tape the two pieces of porcelain together to prevent any possible movement. If, after removal of the two final rivets (and the tape), the two pieces will not come apart, it is more than likely that they have also been stuck together; you will then have to try the solvents in order of strength, as described earlier in this chapter (*see pp. 33–7*).

Tying and lacing

Both these processes involve the use of lead solder to join the two ends of the wire together; by cutting through the soldered area you can expose the ends of the wire and unravel the lacing. You can use the same technique for the 'tie': file through the soldered joint and pull the wire through the drill holes. In cases where the restorer has painted over the soldered area to disguise it (a common practice with this method), it may be necessary to remove the paint first in order to expose the area to be cut.

Dowels

Dowels, 'the hidden enemy' as I like to call them, are concealed within the porcelain or a restored area, or both, and so are often very difficult to detect. If you think that a restored piece may have been dowelled you can confirm your suspicion by arranging to have the object X-rayed; metal dowels should show up clearly (*see opposite and above*), though non-metallic ones may be less obvious. If an X-ray is not possible, you will have to rely on your sense of touch. If, after you have applied your solvent, the adhesive line moves to such an extent that you feel the object should come apart, but the pieces still hold together, then the chances are that you are dealing with a dowel. Unfortunately, this is probably the only warning sign you will get; if you ignore it and try to manipulate the pieces, the dowel is likely to break through the porcelain, causing all sorts of damage.

If you can move the two pieces of porcelain so that you can see the dowel, you will be able to cut it with a piercing-saw. The dowel-packing may then be softened with solvent, picked or drilled away and the dowel pulled out. If there is insufficient play on the pieces, soaking may soften the packing enough for you to be able to pull the pieces gently apart. It is wise to start with acetone in case you are dealing with an iron dowel – water might cause rust staining to occur. Epoxy packing would probably respond to acetone or Nitromors®.

It is always a help to know where dowels are most likely to have been used (though in truth they can be found anywhere): handles are a prime target for dowel restorers, as are arms and legs, stems or any parts that project out from the main body and, in general, any part of the object that is hollow.

Adhesive removal

After dismantling your object you will need to remove all traces of the old adhesive. It is very important to do this, as any left on the edges will cause the joining pieces to be marginally further apart than they would otherwise have been. If there are many more fragments to be added, you are likely to find the object sadly out of alignment by the time you reach the last join. We now also know that if an old adhesive is not completely removed it can cause a new one to yellow more quickly. Cleaning it off thoroughly, although tedious, is thus absolutely essential.

Opinion is divided on the best method of removing troublesome old adhesive – dissolving or cutting. To dissolve an old adhesive you have to soften it by soaking cotton wool swabs in the appropriate solvent and applying them repeatedly along the broken edges; you then either brush it away with a hard toothbrush or scrape it away with a sharp blade. This process may have to be carried out three or four times before all the visible adhesive is removed.

For the other method, cutting, you need to use a surgical scalpel. You should only attempt the cutting method on hard-paste porcelain – a soft-paste body could be susceptible to damage by the blade. Allow the adhesive to reharden after dismantling. Then, holding the fragment carefully between your finger and thumb, gently push the scalpel blade down the broken edge, picking and cutting away the adhesive as you go, always pushing the blade away from yourself and as far away from your fingers as possible. Remember that scalpels are designed to cut flesh, and they will do so if used harshly or incorrectly. A desk lamp can be of help during this process; the adhesive, particularly if it is epoxy resin, will shine under the raking light of the lamp. Better still would be to use a binocular microscope in conjunction with a light.

The one objection raised to this method is that the blade might damage the edge of the porcelain. I have found, in fact, that when dealing with hard-paste the opposite is more often the case – the porcelain tends to blunt the blade of the scalpel; keep an eye open for any black lines along the broken edges, caused by minute fragments of blade deposited on the surface, and remove them with acetone as soon as possible. Be careful not to exert too much pressure; it is all too easy to chip off tiny flakes of glaze along the broken edge. So, as always, proceed with caution.

For years I preferred the cutting method, as I felt that it removed the adhesive more completely. The main drawback of the dissolving process comes with the brushing away, which unfortunately sometimes only causes the softened adhesive to spread into any minute holes along the broken edge, thereby preventing a perfect join when sticking. Originally I believed that cutting the adhesive away removed it completely from these holes; however, after years of experimentation I have come to the conclusion that it does not entirely do so, and that a combination of the two methods works best. First, cut away as much as possible of the old adhesive, and then soften the remainder with solvent and remove it by both brushing and picking. In this way there is less adhesive left to spread along the edge of the porcelain.

Cleaning

Once you have dismantled the object and removed the old adhesive or fill, you must clean all the surfaces thoroughly. Is it necessary, though, to clean every fragment before sticking? The answer is, emphatically, yes. Cleaning is done to remove dirt and grease. Grease attracts dirt and these together cause the black lines that so often appear along the edges of joins made by amateur restorers. We have probably all, at one time or another, done the 'household join', as I call it, fitting broken pieces together without first cleaning the edges to be stuck. Even though these joins look perfect when the edges are placed together without the adhesive, an ugly black line all too often disfigures your restoration soon after sticking. Many people blame the adhesive they used, when they should in fact be blaming themselves for being lazy, for it is more than likely that the dirt and grease came from their own fingers. Grease also affects the strength of a join, as it prevents the adhesive from taking a good grip on the edges of the porcelain. Even if you clean the edges and keep your fingers away from them, they can still pick up dirt, and therefore grease, from airborne dust alone. For this reason, you should always cover your cleaned fragments immediately with a clean cloth or with white tissue paper or place them in a clean, covered box until you are ready to stick them together.

Hints and tips
When cleaning, it is advisable to wear clean rubber gloves. These prevent any dirt being transferred to the porcelain from your hands and stop the skin on your hands from becoming dry.

There are several household products you can use to remove grease and dirt, although some of them – concentrated household bleaches, for example *(see pp. 44–5)* – that appear to work well are actually very dangerous to the object.

Synperonic® 91/6
This is a non-ionic detergent that can be used to wash porcelain. It will remove airborne dust but has little effect on the stubborn dirt and grease that collects on broken edges. It is very good for cleaning objects that have been sitting gathering dust and for general cleaning of porcelain after you have treated it.

Swabbing
Make a 0.5 per cent solution of Synperonic® 91/6 and either tap water or distilled water (use the latter only where the water is not of very good quality or may have a high chemical content). If there is a heavy accumulation of dirt, use a warm solution. Clean the surface with a soft brush or cotton wool dipped in the solution, then remove the soap with clean water applied with white tissue paper and leave the object to dry.

Ariel®/Calgon®
There are many biological detergents available for washing clothes, but Ariel® is the most effective as a porcelain cleaner. In very hard water areas you may have to add a water softener, such as Calgon®. Calgon® can be purchased from supermarkets or hardware stores; many of the big supermarkets sell their own brand. Water softener should never be used on any form of lustreware because it can affect the copper in the colour. Ariel® can also dull the appearance of overglaze enamels, so be careful when cleaning an enamelled object not to use too much detergent, and make sure you rinse it off very thoroughly.

Swabbing
This method is really effective only for surface cleaning. Dissolve a very small amount of Ariel® in warm water. Apply the solution to the object on cotton wool swabs and then rinse it off with clean water before drying the surface with white tissue paper.

Soaking
Use a container large enough to take the porcelain pieces and fill it with warm water. Do not use water hotter than 40°C (104°F) as this would destroy the enzymes, thereby halting the cleaning action. Add 2–3 per cent of water softener if needed, stirring until all the powder has completely dissolved, then do the same with the Ariel®. Submerge the porcelain in the solution, covering it completely; to prevent chipping and flaking, ensure that the edges do not scrape together. Leave the pieces in the solution for 2–4 hours, periodically brushing the edges gently with a medium stencil brush or a toothbrush to help

with the removal of dirt and grease. If you notice any flakes of old adhesive at this stage and they do not respond to brushing, remove them with a scalpel. If, after half a day, the pieces are not as clean as you would wish, give the edges a further gentle brushing and leave for a little longer. If you are still not satisfied, make a second solution and repeat the process. If the dirt is very stubborn, leave the pieces overnight. If the next day they are still not clean, try poulticing.

Poulticing

Use this method on dirty edges that have not responded to the above treatments. Make a slightly stronger solution of Ariel®, adding Calgon® if necessary. Cut strips of cotton wool or white, acid-free blotting paper two layers thick (never use coloured paper, as this could stain the edges). Take the pieces of porcelain from their previous cleaning solution and rinse them. Soak the cotton wool in the solution and place it along the dirty edges, ensuring you get a good contact between it and the porcelain. The cotton wool acts as a poultice, sucking the dirt into itself. Check periodically to see if it is working.

Once they are clean, wash the pieces very thoroughly in water. This is best done by putting them into a bowl and running water over them for an hour or so, or by leaving them to soak in water for several hours, then giving them a final rinse. It cannot be sufficiently stressed how important it is to remove all traces of detergent; experience has shown that any residue of cleaning agents left in the body of a ceramic object can have an adverse effect on the adhesive or filler used later. Now blot the pieces with clean tissues to remove the surface water and lay them out to dry.

Hydrogen peroxide and ammonia

Hydrogen peroxide (H_2O_2) with a few drops of ammonia added is one of the most effective cleaning agents for porcelain. Recently, however, a few problems have been encountered, especially with soft-paste porcelain, when objects

Hints and tips
Hydrogen peroxide can decompose in its container in the presence of sunlight and/or heat, and if it is left uncovered it can easily revert to water within just one to two days. Make sure you replace the cap securely on the bottle after use, and store it in a cool, dark place.

Take care
Do take particular care if you are using hydrogen peroxide and ammonia to clean a gilded object, especially if the gilding appears unstable. The ammonia could affect any gilding that is not pure gold. On one occasion I was cleaning such an object and the solution caused the gilding to lift from it. (Sometimes, of course the apparently original gilding turns out to be a skilful restoration, as it was in this case.)

previously cleaned with the peroxide solution and subsequently stuck with one of the specialized epoxies have had the joins turn yellow very quickly. This could be because the peroxide residue has not been washed out properly. We are not really sure what long-term effects residual hydrogen peroxide and ammonia could have on the restoration materials or on the ceramic itself. To be on the safe side, therefore, you should not consider using a solution of peroxide and ammonia on anything other than hard-paste porcelain.

You can get hold of hydrogen peroxide readily – in fact, you can buy it over the counter at any chemist shop in two strengths: 30 volume and 20 volume. However, the 100 (30 per cent) volume is obtainable only from chemical suppliers. It should then be diluted before use to 20 volume, which is the strength that I find works best.

The peroxide is used in conjunction with a very small quantity of ammonia (really just a few drops, no matter how much peroxide is being used). The ammonia plays no part in the cleaning action; it acts only as a catalyst, releasing the spare oxygen in the solution, which then joins with the dirt and grease and brings them to the surface of the broken edges of the porcelain. Unfortunately, the ammonia can also oxidize any iron in the body of the object into its ferric form, causing yellow/brown staining to appear.

It should not be necessary to use hydrogen peroxide at all if you obtain good results with a solution of Ariel®/Calgon®, but you can use it as a last resort if the ingrained dirt and grease prove to be very stubborn.

Poulticing
Place the fragments to be cleaned into water for a few minutes to reduce any absorption of the peroxide into the body. When you remove them, blot with white tissue paper to remove the surface water. Make up strips of paper tissue 2.5cm (1in) wide and three layers thick, or use cotton wool (but then you must make sure that no small strands of cotton fibre are left clinging to the edges of the porcelain after removal). Soak your swab in the peroxide and, using a pair of tweezers or wearing thin rubber gloves to protect your fingers, place it along the broken edges, making a good contact by tamping it down with a stencil brush, then cover it with tinfoil. Ideally, renew the hydrogen peroxide swabs every two hours. I usually start this process in the morning, in the hope that the porcelain will be clean by mid-afternoon. Once the cleaning has been completed, soak the fragments in water overnight to neutralize the cleaning agent. Then lay them out to dry on a clean surface.

Household bleach
The term 'household bleach' applied in this context refers to those concentrated bleaches normally used to clean drains and lavatories; these were often used in the past by restorers to bleach out dirt and stains in porcelain. In fact, it was not an uncommon practice for restorers to leave porcelain fragments to soak in a

bleach solution. Do not, under any circumstances, be fooled by the admittedly good – sometimes even spectacular – results that can be achieved through the use of household bleaches, because there are hidden dangers. You must always bear in mind that you are not cleaning an intact object; any solution that is used will enter the body of the porcelain through the broken edges. If the bleach is not completely removed through continuous washing or prolonged soaking in water (which is an almost impossible task), it will remain in the body and eventually form crystals that are likely to appear along the join lines, or anywhere else on the surface where the body is exposed. This is most likely to occur on a foot ring or through any faults that are present in the glaze, such as firing cracks or crazing. The crystals can even cause the glaze to flake off as they form. It is often weeks after the restoration has been completed that these unfortunate effects start to appear – frequently after the object is back with the owner – so I would advise strongly against the use of concentrated bleaches.

ABOVE The discoloured and cracked Laponite® poultice on the back of this Chinese plate is ready for removal.

Laponite® R.D.

This is a synthetic, inorganic colloid in the form of a very fine white powder, which forms a colourless thixotropic gel when it is mixed with a liquid. You should wear a mask when mixing it. It is applied as a poultice and, if it works, it will draw the stain out of the body, as opposed to hydrogen peroxide, which will only bleach it.

Poulticing

Add 3–5 per cent of Laponite® to water, mix it in and leave it to stand in an airtight container for three to four hours, until it forms a gel; meanwhile soak the object in water for up to two hours. Apply the Laponite® to the affected area with a spatula to a thickness of 3–4mm (about ⅛in). Cover the treated area with clingfilm to slow down evaporation – if you do not take this precaution, the Laponite® will dry too quickly. As the gel dries out it will crack and shrink to about 50 per cent of its original volume; it should also draw out some of the stain/dirt, which will appear as a colour change in the gel (see above right). You must remove the Laponite® when it is firm, but do not allow it to dry too hard; because of the shrinkage, it can exert considerable pressure as it dries. For this reason, it is not recommended for use on the edges or surfaces of fragile objects. Wash the object with water to remove any Laponite® residue.

If you wish to incorporate a solvent other than water – for example, you may want to use IMS to remove any shellac that may be present on the porcelain – you must first mix the Laponite® with water and add the solvent only once the gel has formed.

Steam cleaning

Steam has been used very effectively for many years to clean stone, and more recently this same idea has been adopted for use on ceramics. The steam cleaners I have used are the Derotor GV and GV6 models, 3- and 5-litre (5¼- and 8-pint) capacity, respectively. Distilled water is preferable, to avoid a build-up of limescale deposits.

How to use
First, fill the boiler with water and switch it on. Depending on the type and capacity, it will take about twenty minutes to reach boiling point. Next, apply the steam to the object using the hand nozzle, which has a built-in push-button control. You can regulate the pressure by adjusting a separate valve and also by the distance you hold the nozzle from the object.

Steam cleaning can be a very effective treatment for removing ingrained dirt or adhesive from the broken edges of porcelain (*see p. 34*), but you should not use it on fragile or damaged surfaces. If used with caution it is often a successful method for cleaning open cracks.

Putty rubber; Groom/stick® (dry cleaning)

Both of these products can be effectively used by restorers to clean the surface of unglazed ceramics, such as Wedgwood or Parian ware, as an alternative to wet cleaning the porcelain. A putty rubber looks like an ordinary eraser but is softer; Groom/stick® is bought in sheets like Blu-tack®. They are both off-white in colour and can be rolled or rubbed over the object to lift and remove the surface dirt. Because of their malleability, you can break off convenient-sized pieces and then stretch or mould them into suitable shapes for cleaning awkward areas.

Stain removal

Stains can be either organic in nature, usually resulting from day-to-day use, or inorganic, most likely caused by either metal supports (for example, rivets) that have been used on the outside of the porcelain (*see p. 16–19*) or metal dowels within the body of the porcelain, or a combination of both.

Stains along cracks or in the body of a piece (*see opposite*) are in many cases impossible to remove completely, and often you must content yourself with reducing their disfiguring effect to a minimum. It is even possible to make the staining worse because once the object is wetted the stains become mobile and may disperse further into the body rather than being drawn out.

You may be lucky enough to be able to remove organic staining completely by repeatedly soaking the object in an Ariel® and water solution or by repeated applications of a Laponite® poultice; the latter technique has proved extremely successful on badly stained glazed earthenware.

There are a few commercial iron stain removers on the market, such as Jenolite® (phosphoric acid), but these are strong chemicals to bring into contact with porcelain and you cannot be certain that you will wash all the chemical residue out after the treatment.

Copper stains are usually dark green in colour and do not occur naturally in the body of the porcelain; they normally come from dowels or from gilt-bronze ornamentation. Unfortunately, these stains are even more difficult to remove than iron stains. The only treatment that is likely to have any effect is as follows. Put on safety goggles and protective gloves before soaking a cotton wool pad in a strong solution of ammonia. Press this pad over the stained area, cover it with tinfoil and leave it overnight. Then wash the porcelain using the Ariel®/Calgon® method (see pp. 42–3).

With all methods of cleaning you need to make sure that the porcelain body is completely dry before proceeding to the next stage. Place the object or the fragments on white tissue paper (not coloured paper or newspaper, as the colour or newsprint is likely to transfer itself to the edges) and allow to dry naturally. The fragments will need to be covered while drying for protection against dust; white tissue paper loosely draped over the top should suffice. There are two more things to bear in mind: first, do not touch the edges that have just been cleaned and, second, be prepared for the drying process to take much longer than you expect. Once the fragments are thoroughly dry they are ready for sticking. If you do not intend to do the job immediately, it is essential to keep them clean. A sandwich tray with a tight-fitting plastic lid or cover is ideal for this purpose.

LEFT A detail of an eighteenth-century English porcelain mug showing a badly stained crack.

4 Reconstruction

Once the porcelain fragments have been cleaned and are completely dry, your next task is to decide on how you will stick them back together. In order to do this, you will have to find answers to three separate questions, before you even make a start on the joining process:

1 Which way do the fragments fit together?
2 Which is the best adhesive to use?
3 Which method are you going to use to join the fragments?

Contrary to popular belief, reconstructing a porcelain object is not just a process of sticking one fragment to another until the job is done.

Basic reconstruction

The first of the questions above is sometimes a lot more difficult to answer than it appears, and taking the wrong course can lead to total failure. If you want to avoid having to start the whole job over again, do not just join any two pieces together and continue sticking in the hope that all the pieces will fit perfectly in the end. It is likely that at some stage you will find at least one piece – in a complex reconstruction, perhaps several pieces – 'trapped out', as we term it. In other words, the pieces do not align precisely, or do not fit at all.

The illustration of a broken plate (*see below*) illustrates just such a problem. The plate has a large 'master' fragment **A** and two minor fragments **B** and **C**. Master fragments may not always be the largest – more important than size is that they should have retained the overall shape of the piece to be restored, and should not have 'sprung' (*see p. 63*). Even with only three pieces to stick, there are several possibilities:

BELOW The sticking sequence for a broken plate: A = master fragment; B and C = minor fragments. It is the D and E points, in particular, that could create problems if you chose the wrong sequence. As explained in the accompanying text, the correct sequence is B to C, then this complex to A.

Possibility 1 Stick **B** and **A** together, allow the join to cure, then add **C**. This would certainly be the wrong sequence, as fragment **C** would be badly trapped out by the sharp cut-back in the **C/B** join, the very tight junction at point **D** and the curve at **E**, which would prevent piece **C** from even reaching the junction at **D**.

Possibility 2 Stick **B** to **C**, allow the join to cure, then stick this new large fragment to **A**. This choice is definitely better than the first, but still has one major hazard – it would be all too easy to get the join between **B** and **C** slightly wrong, with the result that the new fragment would not marry with piece **A**.

Possibility 3 It would be much better to stick **C** to **A**, allow the join to cure, and then stick fragment **B** to the **A/C** composite. For less experienced restorers, this could be the best course of action, as it would avoid some of the pitfalls, though point **D** would still be a possible worry.

Possibility 4 – the correct solution The correct solution would be to stick all the fragments together at the same time, before the adhesive has had time to cure, in either of these sequences: **C** to **A** and then **B**, or **C** to **B** and then this composite fragment to the large piece **A**. Simultaneous assembly allows you to make adjustments to all three fragments at once in order to achieve a perfect fit.

Complex reconstruction

For more complicated reconstructions involving many fragments you would be wise to attempt a trial assembly, known as a 'dry run', using tape instead of adhesive. I generally use white masking tape for this purpose because it is easy to see and is also less sticky and thus easier to remove. However, if the porcelain object is very large and heavy it is a better idea to use Sellotape®, which is stronger. Use the tape in the same way as you would if you were actually sticking the object (*see pp. 59–62*).

Making a trial assembly

The images that follow (*see pp. 50–1*) show a Chinese vase, approximately a third of which has been broken into fragments – the type of repair routinely encountered by porcelain restorers. The captions explain step by step how I assembled this piece.

When making a trial assembly, it makes sense to number each fragment, once fitted, in the order in which you added it to the complex. Write each number on a small piece of masking tape and fix it to the surface of the fragment. In this way, when you come to the sticking stage you do not have to rely on memory but will be able to see which piece follows which. If you have chosen to stick your numbers to the inside faces of, say, a narrow-necked object, as I did with the vase illustrated, don't forget to remove them while they are still accessible.

During the sticking process always bear in mind the length of time you will have in which to make your joins (which will depend on the type of adhesive you have chosen to use). Remember, too, that you must not touch the edges of the fragments (otherwise all the time you have spent cleaning them will be wasted), and that you must not grate the edges together, as by doing so you risk dislodging small flakes of glaze.

1 I took this piece as the master fragment. It is easier to build up from the base or to invert an object and build up from the neck, even if the largest fragment is a side piece.

2 This v-shaped fragment seemed the most obvious one to fit first to the master fragment.

3 I secured the fragment with tape and numbered it 2 (number 1 being the master fragment).

4 For my next piece, I looked for a straight line or gentle curve – these are less likely to cause trap-outs. In fact, though, a trap-out was created by the very next piece that I tried.

5 To avoid the trap-out, I decided to fit a smaller piece instead, labelling it 3.

6 When I tried again to fit the piece shown in step 4, it still created a troublesome trap-out.

7 The solution was to attach two small pieces, 4a and 4b, to the large piece, which I numbered 4, and then to fit this assembly to the complex.

8 The next piece to be fitted to the complex was this large rim fragment, which I labelled 5.

9 Fragment 6 was also part of the rim, but it formed a slightly angled cut-back.

10 To avoid this potential trap, I decided to attach a triangular-shaped piece, labelled 6a, to fragment 6 first.

11 The small missing area on the horse's head was filled by two small fragments fitted together, 7a and 7b.

(Private collection)

12 The vase was completed by a single large rim fragment, labelled 8, leaving a few missing chips along some of the joins, which would need filling (*see Chapter 5*) once the joins had been stuck.

Adhesives

Once you have made the trial assembly of your piece, you must decide on your method of joining (*see pp. 57–9*) and choose your adhesive. Remember always to follow health and safety regulations when using adhesives.

It is in the field of adhesives that we come closest to having the 'ideal' material for porcelain restoration (*see box below left*). For some time now, adhesives have been available that fulfil most of our requirements, but in recent years at least four new ones have been developed that fit the bill almost perfectly. They are discussed under 'Specialized epoxy resins' (*see pp. 55–7*).

Adhesives are generally classed according to their chemical make-up; I shall confine my discussion to four types: cellulose nitrate, acrylic resins, cyano-acrylates and epoxy resins. The most widely used are the epoxies; virtually every manufacturer produces at least one of this type. The following section discusses the pros and cons of some of the adhesives most often used on porcelain.

Cellulose nitrate
HMG®
I often call this the 'showcase' adhesive, as it tends to be used only if the porcelain is not going to be frequently handled or washed. (In fact, no repaired piece should be regarded as safe for domestic use, even if it has been mended with the strongest available adhesive.) It is water-white in colour and has the advantage that it does not discolour for some time. It is easy to use and sets by the loss of a solvent, and therefore does not cause any of the problems that can occur with more complex adhesives. Cellulose nitrate dissolves easily in acetone even after it has cured. Because it is not one of the very strong adhesives, it is not widely used on porcelain, but it is perfectly suitable for the repair of porous earthenware. It can also be used as a consolidant for plaster of Paris (*see pp. 93–4*). Pure cellulose nitrate tends to become brittle with age, but HMG® has an added plasticizer that makes it more stable.

Acrylic resins
Paraloid® B72; B72 Restoration Adhesive
This is an adhesive very similar to cellulose nitrate in properties and application, but it is a little thicker and tends to form bubbles as it cures. It is said to be stronger, and may be so, but I find it difficult to handle (perhaps because I am so much more used to cellulose nitrate). It also has the nasty habit of going stringy. Paraloid® B72 comes in the form of dried beads, which can be dissolved in acetone to the consistency you require; it is also available in tubes sold as B72 Restoration Adhesive. Both forms are obtainable from specialist suppliers. If you are making up your own, it is a good idea to add IMS once the Paraloid® has nearly dissolved, to reduce the volatility of the acetone. A suitable ratio is 30–50g (1–1¾oz) of Paraloid® to 100ml (3⅓ fl oz) of acetone and IMS in equal parts.

The 'ideal' adhesive
In order to qualify as 'ideal', an adhesive must have the following properties:
• It must be strong enough to stick any porcelain object securely, however large.
• Its consistency should be thin enough to give a tight join.
• It should be clear and remain so over a long period.
• It should cure reasonably quickly, but not so fast as to allow no time to realign the fragments if necessary.
• It should be easy to dissolve, or at least to soften enough for the object to be dismantled, and then be removable from the edges of pieces that have been joined, and should remain so even after several years.

Cyanoacrylates

Super glue

These form the group known as impact adhesives – in other words, those that bond immediately when force is applied to the join. (Full cure is not actually reached until a few hours after use.) Although at first sight they seem very effective, they do have a number of disadvantages, the greatest of which is that the restorer has very little time, if any, to align the fragments with the accuracy demanded for porcelain restoration. Another drawback is that they lose strength after long exposure to light and so break down after a few years. They may, however, be used in conjunction with a slower-curing adhesive to tack fragments together in cases where it is necessary to avoid the use of tape – if the object has a delicate surface, for example. This process is known as 'combination' joining (*see p. 58*). Misalignment of the fragments is not necessarily a disaster; cyanoacrylates can be softened with acetone if it is applied immediately.

Epoxy resins

These are the adhesives most widely used by porcelain restorers. Most of the major manufacturers have for many years made at least one epoxy adhesive aimed at the mass market, but the more recent specialized epoxies that have been developed specifically for porcelain and glass restoration have proved even more effective. As a result of their introduction, our whole approach to the use of epoxies has changed.

Let us, therefore, evaluate the most suitable of the available epoxies, dividing them into two groups: those made for general use and the specialized resins designed for the restoration market.

General-use epoxy resins

Although these are used less and less by restorers nowadays, they do still have their place. They formed the basis of modern porcelain repair and in the right hands will produce a more than acceptable result. They can still be used where it is impossible to obtain the relatively new specialized materials. The strongest adhesive and the various fast-setters are still to be found among the popular range of commercial epoxies.

Araldite®

This product was for years the most widely used epoxy resin; indeed, for some time it was the only one available. It consists of a whitish resin and a yellow hardener which, when mixed together in equal parts, make a very strong adhesive. It is, in my opinion, undoubtedly the strongest commercially available epoxy suitable for porcelain restoration. Its colour, when mixed, is a milky yellow and its consistency rather thick; this thickness is, in fact, one of its drawbacks. Once mixed it is usable for about two hours. The curing time, depending on room temperature, is between six and twelve hours for handling, and between twenty-four and seventy-two hours for complete curing. It is possible to shorten the process to between one and six hours by heating the mixed resin under a desk lamp until it turns a lighter colour and becomes runny; the thinner consistency will also ensure a tighter join. There are two problems with this method, however. One is that it may weaken the long-term strength of the resin; the other is that yellowing (which occurs anyway) happens much sooner than it otherwise would. If you are after a fast-setting adhesive, therefore, ordinary Araldite® is not the one to choose.

The yellowing of this adhesive can be so strong that it will sometimes show through the paint layers of a repair. In anticipation of the problem, some restorers have tried to prevent it by adding white pigment to the resin mix. This, however, can weaken the epoxy, and if you add too much pigment (easy to do) you will find that the resin will not stick properly. I believe that the strength of the join is all-important, and would therefore advise against adding pigment, especially in view of the vastly improved covering qualities of modern paints and painting mediums. If you experience weak joins when using Araldite®, or indeed other epoxies, the cause may be the age of the adhesive (*see p. 57*).

Araldite® AY 103 with hardener HY 956

This was probably the first of the more liquid adhesives. It comes in 500g packs from specialist suppliers and consists of a water-white resin (AY 103) and a hardener (HY 956), which has a yellow tint. Unlike conventional epoxy resins it is mixed in a ratio by volume of 100 parts resin to 18–20 parts hardener (or approximately 5:1). Restorers used to use an eye-dropper or a syringe to measure the components, but disposable plastic pipettes are now available that are specifically designed for the purpose. Alternatively, you may use small digital scales and measure by weight, in which case the ratio will be 100 parts resin to 16–18 parts hardener. When mixed, AY 103/HY 956 has a very thin, runny consistency, which ensures a tight join. It is usable for about three and a half hours but its setting time varies considerably depending on room temperature and the accuracy of the mixing. Normally, it takes about three hours to harden enough for handling and is completely cured in twenty-four hours. Like so many other epoxies, the cured resin yellows after a short period and can be affected by humidity if it is badly mixed. The hardener gradually yellows in the bottle, so it should be replaced after one year. I personally use this resin now more as a casting material (*see p. 94*) than as an adhesive.

Fast-setting epoxy resins

There are many fast-setting epoxy resins on the market, with a wide range of different properties. While they do have their uses, they are weaker than the normal epoxies. Beginners are often flustered by them; I think it is the word 'fast' that causes them to rush the joining process – often with disastrous results. Although the products that harden in two to three minutes can catch you out, those that take at least five to fifteen minutes to harden should give you ample time for correct alignment. Two of these are discussed below.

Super Epoxy
This is a water-white, fast-setting epoxy resin with a setting time of five to ten minutes at room temperature. An object repaired with this adhesive can be handled after half an hour. It is reasonably strong, with a thin consistency that ensures a good, tight join, and is very easy to use, being a mixture of equal parts of resin and hardener. It does suffer from the problem of yellowing with age, although it is by no means the worst offender in this respect.

Araldite® Rapid
This has many of the characteristics of ordinary Araldite®, consisting of a resin and a hardener that you combine in equal parts. When mixed, it is a milky yellow in colour. At room temperature its setting time is about ten minutes; it hardens in thirty minutes to an hour and reaches full strength in eight hours. When I first started using this resin I found it difficult to handle. It is very thick, so you must take great care not to apply too much to the broken edges or they will not join tightly enough. Araldite® Rapid is used mainly for its speed in setting and for its strength – it is stronger than Super Epoxy. Like the other general-use epoxies, it yellows with age.

Specialized epoxy resins

In recent years, epoxies designed especially for the porcelain restorer have, it seems, eliminated the worst of the problems associated with the general-use adhesives. They are basically very water-white and retain this property for a very long time – exactly what was wanted. It is now possible, if the cleaning and the alignment are perfect, to create a join that is almost invisible. Of course there are, as always, disadvantages: they are expensive, difficult to use because of their low viscosity, slow to cure fully and really do need to be mixed very accurately (*see p. 60*). But if you persevere with them (for at first it will undoubtedly be tempting to go back to the older, easier resins) you will become more adept at handling them. Four resins in this category are Hxtal® NYL-1, Araldite® 2020 (Ciba-Geigy® XY 396/HY 397), Fynebond® and Epo-tek® 301.

Hxtal® NYL-1
This water-white epoxy resin comes in two parts – a resin and a hardener – which are mixed in a ratio of 3 parts resin to 1 part hardener by weight. At room temperature the mixed resin takes twenty-four hours to stiffen and another six days to cure fully. It gives an extremely strong bond and its low viscosity permits a very tight join as well as allowing it to penetrate cracks better than any other adhesive I have used before. When age-tested, this resin took an extraordinarily long time to show any signs of yellowing. It is for this reason

Take care
HMG® cellulose nitrate used in close proximity to Hxtal® and the other specialized adhesives can cause yellowing, as can some cleaning chemicals, particularly hydrogen peroxide, if not washed out properly. Do not use Sellotape® as an aid to sticking, as there is a reaction at the point of contact that turns the resin violet; use Magic® tape instead.

Warning
Hxtal® and Araldite®
2020 both contain an
amine in the hardener
that is toxic until the
components are
thoroughly blended,
so make sure you wear
a mask or use a fume
cupboard when
mixing them.

Hints and tips
If you are sticking a
piece of soft-paste
porcelain with a
specialized epoxy resin
it is better to allow the
adhesive to cure slightly
until it gels before
applying it to the
broken edge. If you use
it straight away there is
a risk that it could seep
into the body of the
object and stain it. The
specialized resins can
also be used as fillers if
bulking agents are
added (see pp. 74–6).

that we have persevered despite the difficulties of using it. In comparison with general-use epoxies it is expensive, so you are advised not to mix more than is necessary, although the working life of mixed resin can be extended by a few days if you keep it in the ice-making compartment of your refrigerator.

The biggest disadvantage Hxtal® lies in its curing time: seven days. The manufacturer has said that it is possible to reduce this by warming the resin; we have found, though, that once the resin has cured, excessive heating – for example, with a hot-air blower – dramatically hastens the onset of yellowing. To be on the safe side it is probably wise to avoid heating at any stage.

Araldite® 2020 (resin XW 396 and hardener XW 397)
This water-white epoxy resin is the cheapest of the specialized epoxies. It is very similar to Hxtal®, having two components that you mix in a ratio of 3 parts resin to 1 part hardener by weight, being equally strong and having very good penetrative qualities when used on a crack. The main difference between them is that at room temperature Araldite® 2020 gives you about forty-five minutes' working time, takes only twenty-four hours to harden enough for handling and cures fully in three days; it is also more liquid than Hxtal®. When tested by accelerated ageing it yellowed slightly quicker than Hxtal®, but there was little to choose between them in this respect. On curing, however, Araldite® 2020 is not as hard as Hxtal® and when used to fill shallow chips it has a tendency to flake away at the edges.

Fynebond®
This is the most recent water-white epoxy resin to appear on the market. It was developed to take the place of Ablebond, which is no longer available and to which it is very similar. It again has two components that you mix in a ratio of 3 parts resin to 1 part hardener by weight. Its curing time is very close to that of Araldite® 2020 – if anything, slightly shorter. Although it does not give quite as strong a bond as the other two, it does cure as hard as Hxtal®. When submitted to accelerated ageing tests it yellowed slightly quicker than either Hxtal® or Araldite® 2020. This resin has the drawback of crystallizing in the bottle; if you warm it gently (as recommended on the label) it will revert to a semi-liquid state, and should remain so for about forty-eight hours before recrystallizing. Warming, however, could possibly accelerate the yellowing process.

Epo-tek® 301
This water-white adhesive, which was originally developed for use with optical filters but is now also used by porcelain restorers, is similar in properties to the other three. It is mixed in a ratio of 4 parts resin to 1 part hardener by weight. Its viscosity is very low, it cures to an extremely strong and hard bond at room temperature and it has excellent resistance to yellowing. Epo-tek® 301 does, however, crystallize in the bottle and so, like Fynebond®, needs to be heated.

Although all four resins give a good, strong join, they will do so only if the mixing is correct. Accuracy in measuring these specialized adhesives is vital. Even the slightest error could create a weak join or even prevent the resin from curing properly. To ensure success, therefore, you are strongly advised to use a pair of digital scales. A damp atmosphere can also adversely affect the curing properties of these, or indeed any other, adhesives.

Joining methods

There are essentially six techniques used for joining broken porcelain. Four are used to repair what I call straightforward breaks and the other two are used for dealing with damage caused by cracks and 'springing' (*see pp. 62–3*).

Straightforward joining

The four methods for repairing a broken piece of porcelain are single joining, multiple joining, combination joining and the latest method, now possible following the introduction of the specialized epoxy resins, capillary joining.

Single joining

This involves, as its name would suggest, joining one fragment of porcelain at a time to the main complex. Secure each join with tape and allow it to dry partly before adding the next piece. The advantages with this process are that you have plenty of time to align the joins perfectly and that you can leave a join to set, confident that it will not be disturbed by the addition of the next fragment. If you wish to speed up the overall process, you can always use a fast-setting epoxy. This is a good method if there are not too many fragments to be joined, and is the best for beginners, with one proviso: you have to be absolutely precise in fitting each new fragment to the main complex, for one small misalignment at the outset will be greatly magnified by the final stages.

Multiple joining

This involves joining the fragments one after another without waiting for each join to cure. Use Sellotape® (if you are not using a specialized epoxy) or Magic® tape to hold the joins together during the curing period. The advantages of this method are in its speed and in the ability it gives you to make fine adjustments when all the pieces are in place but before the adhesive has cured, and so correct any misalignments. It is not advisable to use a fast-setting adhesive, as you do not want any one of the joins to set before you have inserted the last fragment. It is best not to attempt this method until you are competent at the single-joining method, as dealing with a number of fragments at the same time can pose the same problems as juggling with tennis balls – two or three are not too difficult, but each additional ball calls for a new level of expertise. With the

Epoxy shelf-life

Most adhesives and resins, if bought direct from the manufacturer, have a shelf-life of about two to three years. If you buy them from a retailer, however, there is no guarantee that they will last this long. In my experience, the strength of epoxy resins definitely diminishes with age. I noticed this tendency particularly when I bought a large quantity of adhesive, which I then kept in stock for some time. Buy small amounts and mark the date of purchase on each packet.

multiple joining method you might find yourself dealing with ten, fifteen or even more pieces at the same time, so it is certainly not a technique to be recommended for beginners.

Combination joining

This is used for very heavy objects or for fragments that are both awkward to support and need strength in their joins, such as arms, legs and handles. These objects require the strongest possible adhesive and, in addition, a 'tacking' adhesive to secure the joins during the curing process (tape on its own not being strong enough to provide the necessary support). The procedure is exactly the same as for the single and multiple join, except that you use a strong adhesive, such as Araldite®, in tandem with one of the impact adhesives, such as Loctite® super glue. You spread the Araldite® along the central part and on each end of the broken edge, leaving two small areas free of adhesive. To these areas, add a small spot of the impact adhesive, leaving enough room for it to spread, and press the two fragments firmly together. Be sure to align them perfectly, because the impact adhesive will set immediately, giving you no time for adjustment. It will then hold the fragments in place while the slower-curing but stronger epoxy cures. This method is also useful on objects with delicate surfaces – unstable gilding, for example – that would be affected by tape. In this case, instead of taping, apply several dots of the impact adhesive along one broken edge, press the two pieces firmly together and then introduce a specialized epoxy by the capillary method. Remember not to use HMG® (cellulose nitrate) with specialized epoxy, for the combination will cause the epoxy to turn yellow very quickly.

Capillary joining

This is a method for which the specialized, low-viscosity resins are ideally suited. First, tape the fragments together across the joins at intervals using Magic® tape – not Sellotape® because of the risk of the reaction already mentioned (*see p. 55*). If the object is large, you may have to apply the tape to both faces. It is most important to pull the tape very tight, as it is the only thing holding the fragments together. Once you have satisfactorily assembled all the pieces, apply the resin along the joins, from one face only, and allow it to seep in by capillary action (*see above*). If you do not remove any

> ### Hints and tips
> Before you start sticking (and this rule applies to every other process in porcelain restoration) make sure you have to hand all the materials and tools necessary to complete the operation. There is nothing more annoying, and potentially disastrous, than having to go in search of an essential item while in the middle of a job.

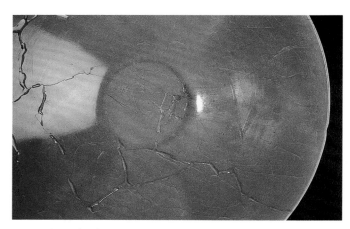

ABOVE Specialized epoxy resin has been applied to all the joins on this Celadon bowl and left to seep in by capillary action.

excess resin straight away, Araldite® 2020 or Fynebond®, although they will be cured enough for handling the next day, can be softened slightly if necessary with acetone applied on a cotton wool swab, and then pared off with a scalpel. If you have used Hxtal®, however, you should leave it for two to three days because of its longer curing time. More resin can be introduced from the other face after curing to any areas that seem to need it.

Procedure for straightforward joining

1 Before starting the sticking process recheck the stability of any surface decoration, such as gilding. You should not use adhesive tape on unstable areas, for obvious reasons. If the gilding appears to be in good condition, you can make the following test: take a tiny piece of tape and fix it lightly over the gilding in the most inconspicuous place you can find. It might be safer to use masking tape which, although not quite as strong or 'stretchy' as other tapes, is less sticky and, therefore, less likely to cause damage. If no gilding is transferred to the tape, press it down more firmly and check again. If the tape comes off clean, you can proceed with caution. To be absolutely sure, however, you may want to make the same test in two or three different places. If any of the gilding is at all unstable, you must keep the tape away from it altogether. There may be no suitable external area on which to put the tape, in which case you may have to content yourself with using it on the inside only. On the rare occasions when this is not possible either – for example, on a bowl that is gilded inside and out – you will probably have to try combination joining instead.

2 You are now ready to apply the adhesive. Before doing so you should have made, if necessary, your trial alignment or 'dry run' (*see pp. 49–51*) of the pieces to be stuck, to get an idea of how well they lock together and the order in which you should assemble them.

3 Take a white tissue or a cotton wool swab, dampen it with acetone and clean the two edges to be stuck, to remove any grease that may have accumulated since you initially cleaned the object. If you use cotton wool, remember to check the edges afterwards in case it has left any fibres on the porcelain. Then clean the glass or tile on which you are going to mix the adhesive. If you don't have a tape dispenser, cut a number of pieces of tape and attach them by one end to the edge of the bench, first making sure that the bench is clean. Try not to touch the sticky side of the tape, to avoid transferring grease from your fingers. You must always cut the tape you require before joining the fragments and place it where you can reach it with one hand only, as your other hand is likely to be holding the fragments to be joined.

4 If you have chosen a one-tube adhesive, the procedure is simple: apply it straight from the tube to the broken edges, or use a cocktail stick to transfer it.

For joining you will need

• A means of supporting the object; the most usual choice is a suitably sized sand box. Make sure you wash the sand clean of any dirt before use.
• White paper tissues – the dye of coloured tissues could be transferred to the object if acetone is used.
• A suitably sized sheet of glass, a watch glass or a glazed tile on which to mix the adhesive.
• A small container of acetone.
• Wooden cocktail sticks.
• Sellotape® or Magic® tape ranging from 0.6–2.5cm (¼–1in) wide – the width chosen will depend on the size of the object to be stuck.
• The adhesive of your choice for the job.

RIGHT Using a pipette ensures accurate measurement of resin. Where 0.5ml is required, for example, take up 1.5ml of the resin and expel until you reach the 1.0ml mark.

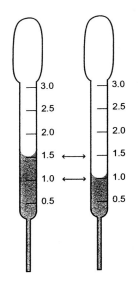

If you are using a two-part adhesive, remove both tubes from the packet together; squeeze the required amount from the resin tube on to the glass, immediately replace the cap and put the tube back into its packet. Then squeeze an equal amount of hardener next to, but not touching, the resin. If you follow this procedure you will not forget which part of the adhesive you have placed on the glass, should you be distracted for some reason. It is all too easy to make a mistake when using water-white epoxies. Then, using a wooden cocktail stick, mix the resin and hardener together with small, even, circular movements, incorporating a little resin and hardener with each movement. Use the gap between the two as your mixing area. It is crucial to ensure that the mix is thorough; it is equally important that the quantities are accurately measured. If you need only a very small amount of mixed adhesive it may be more practical and economical to extract a tiny blob from each tube in turn, remembering to use separate cocktail sticks for resin and hardener.

Hints and tips

The greatest mistake made by beginners is usually to apply far too much resin in the belief that the more adhesive they use the stronger the join will be. Strength in a join actually depends on the right choice of adhesive, according to the type and body of the object, accuracy in mixing the adhesive, the absence of grease and dirt, correct alignment and adequate pressure when joining the fragments. Excessive humidity in the air while curing takes place can also impair the strength of a join.

5 For mixing the specialized resins the above methods are not quite precise enough; you will need to use some form of measuring device. The best is a small set of digital scales, but these are expensive. A cheaper alternative is to use graduated, plastic pipettes, which come in two sizes, larger for the resin and smaller for the hardener. When using pipettes for measuring, it is best to take up more resin into the tube than you require, so that you can more accurately expel the correct amount using the measuring gauge on the side. For example, if you require 0.5ml of resin, take up 1.5ml and expel to the 1ml mark (*see above*). The surplus can then be returned to the bottle. Measure the correct proportion of hardener in a separate pipette, using the same method. As these resins are runnier, a flat glass is not really suitable for mixing them; I generally use a watch glass for the purpose.

6 The essence of any good join is in its tightness and alignment. The only way to ensure a tight bond is to use the adhesive as sparingly as possible. Once you are satisfied that the resin is thoroughly mixed, apply it *to one edge only*, using the cocktail stick. If you are joining two fragments of unequal length, choose the shorter of the two edges so that you are not left with any excess adhesive at either end of your join. Apply it along the centre of the edge only, leaving a little space at each end of the fragment, to allow the resin to spread over the whole area to be stuck without oozing out when the pieces are joined. If you have applied too much, run a clean cocktail stick along the join to remove the surplus. Alternatively, use a tissue dampened with acetone. One reasonably firm

wipe should be enough; any more and you run the risk of allowing acetone to penetrate the join and weaken the bond between adhesive and porcelain. As well as being sparing with the adhesive, you need a fair degree of strength in your wrists to apply enough controlled pressure to ensure an even spread on to both edges. If you do not have this strength and control, put a thin layer on both edges. Remember, though, that the more adhesive you apply the greater the chances are of inaccurate alignment, with the possibility of an unsatisfactory overall result.

7 When making a join, if possible use the lines of any pattern on the porcelain as a guide. If none exists, align the two fragments visually as best you can and gently ease them into place, applying a little firm pressure as you do so. When exerting pressure always make sure that you push directly towards the other fragment, or the two pieces will be likely to jump apart, causing damage to the glazed edges. Fix a couple of pieces of tape across the join; they should be tight enough to prevent the fragment from falling, but loose enough to allow you to make some adjustment if necessary.

8 Remove excess adhesive, if any, after sticking each new fragment so that you can handle the object without getting adhesive all over your fingers, and thereby all over the porcelain. You will also be able to see clearly whether the front and back faces are properly aligned, and you can further check the front-to-back alignment by passing your fingernail across the join at intervals. You will be able to feel a slight step if the fragments are out of alignment; adjust them as necessary until the step disappears.

9 You now need to make the join more secure. Take a strip of tape, apply it firmly to one of the joined fragments at one end, stretch it across the join and fix it firmly to the other fragment. Then recheck your alignment. Take another strip and attach it in a similar manner at the other end of the join. Two more strips should be applied to the back of the joined fragments, directly opposite the ones you applied to the front. (Depending on the size of the object, the loose tape may be removed at this stage to allow room for the new tape.) The strips of tape hold the fragments in place while the adhesive is curing and, because they are under tension, also help to pull them together. It is important to stretch all your pieces of tape to the same degree; unequal tension can cause the fragments to shift out of alignment. Positioning the strips exactly opposite each other, front and back, can reduce the chances of this happening. To be on the safe side, check the join once or twice during curing.

10 When you are completely satisfied with the join, place the fragments upright in the sand box, using a separating sheet of clingfilm or white tissue paper to prevent contact with the sand. If, however, you are using the 'multiple joining'

method, continue to add the other fragments, following the same procedure for each one and checking constantly the alignment of all the fragments. When you have fitted the last piece, recheck all the joins and make any final adjustments that may be required. You may have to remove some tape in order to do this, but do make sure that you replace it again before leaving the joins to cure.

11 If you are using the capillary method, run the resin along the join on one face only using a suitable implement, such as a cocktail stick, and leave it to seep in. If the object permits, you should place it as flat as possible to prevent the adhesive from running over the surface. (It is easy to apply too much when first attempting this method.) If part of the join is not on the flat, apply the resin to the flat part only, and then wait for a few hours before turning the object to expose the untreated area and run in more resin. Adhesive may, at times, find its way through the join to the other side and drip down the surface of the porcelain. Although this is a good indication that it has penetrated thoroughly, you should remove it with a cocktail stick before it is fully cured, otherwise the excess could stick the object to the bench. As a safeguard, you could place a sheet of greaseproof paper under the object. If, however, the adhesive has not penetrated the join completely, you can apply more from the other side (after curing, to minimize the risk of air pockets).

Cracks

Cracks are a common problem. In the past, restorers either completed the break or drilled a hole at the base of the crack in an attempt to release the tension. Neither of these methods is to be recommended.

There are essentially two types of crack: the 'open', which, when eased apart, allows the tip of a small spatula to be inserted at the top, thereby holding the crack open; and the 'closed', which is not directly accessible and is, therefore, more difficult to deal with.

Repairing an open crack is relatively simple. First, carry out a cleaning process; normally this would be by poulticing or possibly using a steam cleaner (with caution). Make sure that the body of the object is completely dry before continuing to the next stage. Hold the crack open with a spatula and introduce your adhesive. If you have used hydrogen peroxide to clean an open or closed crack – especially on soft-paste porcelain (*see pp. 43–4*) – avoid epoxy and use a very thin solution of Paraloid® B72 instead. Then remove the spatula, align the edges and apply tape across the join to keep it firm.

Closed cracks have always been a great problem and many ways of opening them have been tried, including heating the porcelain, which is a risky operation. Since the introduction of specialized epoxies, however, there has been no need to use other methods, as the low viscosity of these adhesives makes them ideal for sticking tight, closed cracks. First, clean the crack by poulticing or steam, and allow the body to dry completely. Then apply the adhesive along the crack on one side of the object only, and leave the piece in a cool room. I have found that Hxtal® will penetrate even the tightest of cracks.

Springing

'Springing' is the term used to describe what happens when a ceramic object loses its original shape through breakage. It is caused by the release of tensions set up inside the object during the firing process. If broken, the porcelain relaxes slightly, just enough to cause a step or ridge when the pieces are put together.

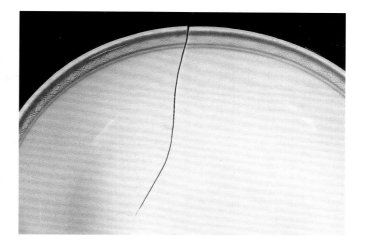

The most obvious sign of springing is a stepped crack on an object; it is also easy to detect on a piece that is broken into only two or three fragments: a plate or bowl is broken in half, for example, and when the two halves are put together they diverge at some point along the join (*see top right*). With objects that have broken into a larger number of fragments, it is more difficult to detect the springing until the sticking process is well under way (one reason why a trial assembly is so important). It is all too easy to blame your own workmanship when you find that the pieces do not join properly.

Sometimes you can align the sprung edges and hold them together with strong tape, but

when the springing is severe, the force needed to push the edges back together and to hold them in position is too great for taping to be effective. In such cases, you have to use not only a strong adhesive but also some type of clamp to hold the pieces in place while the adhesive cures. After trying many methods, most of which were total failures, I developed a double G clamp (*see p. 65*), which, when used with an epoxy of low viscosity, such as Araldite® 2020, works very well indeed. You may be able to make your own clamp, or a version of it in another material, such as wood.

If your porcelain piece is very delicate you may find G clamps rather too heavy, in which case you could use Berna assemblers (carbon fibre clamps) in the same way. They are effective if the springing is not too severe, but would probably be too light to cope with large or heavy pieces.

Before attempting to join the fragments it is essential to find the exact place where the springing starts by putting them together correctly at one end and then passing a fingernail across the join at intervals until you feel the step. Mark

TOP A detail of a porcelain bowl showing a clear example of a sprung join.

ABOVE An end crack clamp (*see p. 65*) being used to hold the sprung join together. (Private collection)

RIGHT Berna assemblers have been used here to exert extra pressure on the joins on an eighteenth-century Qing dynasty *famille rose* vase. (Private collection)

this point on the surface of the porcelain with tape and then, using one of the specialized adhesives, stick the break in the normal way – but only up to the point where the springing starts. Leave the piece until the adhesive is fully cured.

The images on the previous page show a sprung bowl and the same bowl with an end crack clamp in position on either side of the sprung area. (If you are using a double G clamp, you will need to put some padding between the metal heads and the object in order to protect the porcelain.) Slowly and evenly tighten each clamp in turn (one may need to be tightened more than the other), until the two edges come together. Check the alignment with your fingernail.

The clamps should be strong enough to hold the pieces together while you apply the liquid epoxy along the join. Leave the object with the clamps in place until the adhesive has fully cured. When you come to remove the clamps, reduce the pressure slowly on both at the same time. Check the join and shave off any excess adhesive with a scalpel.

An alternative method, if an object is very badly sprung, is to stick the middle area of the join first so that the springing at either end is less pronounced and the strain is eased somewhat. In this case, use two double clamps – one at each end – and then apply the adhesive to both ends in quick succession.

Clamps

There are three types of clamps you should be familiar with. G clamps are simple clamps with a screw action to exert the pressure, and are often all that is needed to give a little extra support to a join. They are made by various manufacturers, in a large range of sizes – the larger they are, the heavier they are, so they may not always be suitable for use on fine porcelain. They are usually made of metal, and the heads will need to be padded to protect the surface of the object under repair.

Berna assemblers (*see above*), which are are very versatile, delicate clamps, are a relatively new idea. They consist of a toughened carbon fibre rod holding two polycarbonate jaws, which move freely on the rod. To the ends of the jaws are fitted silicone rubber buffers, which are very flexible and, therefore,

Take care

Be careful when using clamps; tighten them gradually and cautiously, as any sudden or excess increase in pressure could cause the porcelain to break. If you have already stuck one end, the most vulnerable point will be where the adhesive ends – the risk here will be a break at right angles to the original join.

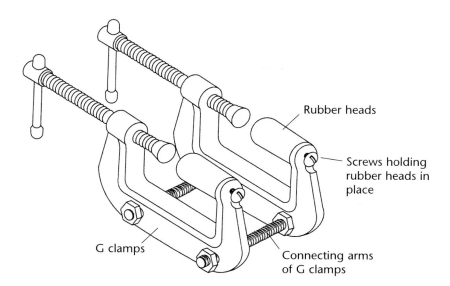

Rubber heads

Screws holding rubber heads in place

G clamps

Connecting arms of G clamps

ABOVE LEFT A purpose-made double G clamp made for use on sprung objects.

sympathetic to the curve of the object (*see opposite*). They give greater control than G clamps because you exert the pressure by squeezing the jaws towards each other. The rods and the jaws are available in different lengths and the jaws can be used in reverse, so that they push two areas apart if you need them to.

End crack clamps (which are very expensive) are precision-made clamps used by stringed musical instrument makers. A few other types of clamp are also produced by this manufacturer, but the one shown here (*see p. 63*) works extremely well for sprung vessels. It is made out of solid aluminium with brass fittings and is strong but very lightweight. You can adjust the angle of the clamping heads to match the curvature of the object by loosening an Allen screw, which can be locked once it is correctly positioned. Even pressure is achieved by adjusting the centrally located tension screw. The clamping heads are cushioned to protect the object.

Additional support

Apart from the types of joins we have been discussing, others, such as arms and handles, sometimes need extra support, in addition to the sand box, while curing. If so, I suggest making a pillar alongside your object using plasticine (but cover it with clingfilm to protect any exposed edges of porcelain from grease – otherwise the adhesive will not stick). Plasticine is fairly hard, yet can easily be moulded into any shape you require. If extra height and strength are needed, plasticine on its own may not be adequate. In such cases, build up a suitable supporting structure from the bench using any convenient rigid materials and mould an appropriately shaped plasticine cradle at the top, covering it with clingfilm. Put the piece to be stuck into this cradle and align the object with it. Lift the fragment out, put the adhesive on the edge, then make the join and rest it once more in the cradle, where it will be supported while the adhesive cures.

5 Replacing missing parts

Most porcelain objects arriving at the restorer's bench have parts missing. They may amount to no more than a few small chips along a broken edge; often, though, arms, flowers, handles or even complete lids may have disappeared, or there may be large areas missing from, say, a dish or the body of a vase. To restore these, you need to be familiar with a variety of materials and techniques.

Backing materials

However small the missing area may be – even if you can barely see daylight through the gap – you will need to use a filling material to replace it, as well as a backing to support the filler while it hardens. And you have to make the backing before even thinking about mixing the resin.

What do you look for in a backing material? First, it must be pliable enough to take on the shape of the missing area; second, it must be strong enough to allow you to push the filling material into place without altering its shape; third, it must be easy to remove; and fourth, it must not, of course, stick to the filler.

Plasticine
In my opinion this is the least effective of the backing materials in general use. Though easily shaped, it is unfortunately equally easy to misshape. It is also very greasy – a property that can have a detrimental effect on the adhesive qualities of the filler.

Adhesive tape
In this category are Sellotape®, masking tape, Magic® tape and Crystal® tape. Adhesive tape can be very effective as a backing if the holes to be filled are very small or if the missing area is on the flat part of an object (the base of a plate, for example). For larger holes, the tape will have to be overlapped to give extra support; even so, you may need to do a lot of reshaping once the filler has hardened because the tape is likely to distort when the filler is applied. Adhesive tape can also be difficult to remove from some types of filler.

Sheet dental wax
This is by far the best option for use as a general-purpose backing material. It comes in sheets approximately 20 x 10cm (7¾ x 4in). As with any other type of wax, you soften it by applying heat – hot water or a hot-air blower (such as a hair dryer). Wax will take up the shape of the surface to be moulded as well as a certain amount of detail; although it is not malleable enough to be suitable for moulding intricate relief details it is excellent for rims of bowls, plates and so

on. It is easy to cut and quick to use, you can readily adjust it once it is in place by heating it with a hot-air blower, and you can remove it without difficulty once the filler has hardened. In addition, two or more sheets can be melted along their edges and joined together if you need to back a large area.

Silicone rubber putty
This fast-setting putty (*see pp. 90–1*), developed fairly recently, is normally used to make detailed moulds, but it works equally well as a backing material. It gives a very smooth and accurate finish to the filler, but because it is rather expensive you may prefer to reserve it for more complicated pieces, such as, for example, a plate with a raised pattern.

Fillers

Depending on whether or not your object is translucent and on the kind of effect you want to achieve, two different options are open to you:

• You can choose a filler that is colour-matched only to the extent that a light-coloured filler is used for white porcelain and a darker one for, say, grey or black stoneware; you will subsequently need to paint these fills.
• You can go for a colour-matched fill using a clear epoxy resin, to which you then add a bulking agent and a colour medium during mixing in order to achieve, if you are skilful, a perfect match with the body colour and/or glaze of the object (*see pp. 74–7*).

Regardless of which method you use, the filling materials will need some degree of shaping and smoothing and so must be easy to work with. In the case of fillers that require painting, there are many suitable ones available and you will probably choose the brand you find easiest to work with; if you opt for a colour-matched fill the choice is more limited. I would advise you to find out by experiment which method and material you are happy with and continue with them until you become expert in their use. The more you chop and change the more likely you are to run into problems.

Fillers that require painting
Epoxy resins
Araldite® 2011 (originally 2001)
When used as a filler, this epoxy is mixed in equal proportions of resin and hardener with the addition of kaolin, which acts as a bulking agent. If you also add a little zinc oxide or titanium dioxide (zinc being cheaper but liable to discolour), the yellow resin will be transformed into a thick, white paste. When you add these materials to the resin you must ensure that they are thoroughly

---

The 'ideal' filler
To qualify as an 'ideal' filler, the product must have the following properties:
• It must have good adhesive qualities – in other words, it must stick firmly to the edges of the porcelain.
• It must be easy to work, and must smooth to a perfectly flat surface without air holes.
• It must accommodate further applications of resin, if necessary.
• It must not shrink.
• It must not be so hard that the tools needed to smooth it would scratch the original glaze.
• If necessary, it must take paint.

incorporated, for any powder left unmixed will cause small holes to appear at the smoothing stage. Araldite® used in this way has good adhesion and does not shrink – in short, it is a very good filler. It can be mixed to any consistency you require: when combined with a high proportion of kaolin it becomes stiff enough to fill very large holes without sagging; with a small amount of kaolin added, it is thin enough to fill small chips along a break line. You can smooth the surface before the fill hardens, using either talc or acetone. I prefer talc, as it has no effect on the resin (unlike acetone, which can soften the surface if you use too much). Choosing a filler is a matter of personal preference; I myself, for some inexplicable reason, do not like the slippery feel of Araldite®. Another slight disadvantage is that it takes a long time to cure in comparison with polyester fillers – about four hours to set and twenty-four hours to cure fully.

Milliput®

This epoxy putty consists of two roll-shaped components; you cut equal amounts from each and mix them together. It has excellent adhesive properties and is very hard when cured. If you find that you prefer to work a hard material, then this may be a suitable filler for you. It is sold in four grades, differentiated by colour – the superfine white is most suitable for porcelain repair. The hardener is slightly yellower than the resin, so it is easy to see when they are thoroughly blended. Kneading by hand is the easiest method. The mixed putty can be modelled easily and smoothed with water, acetone or talc. It dries very hard in two to three hours at room temperature. There is one drawback: it has been observed that when Milliput® is used in conjunction with Rustin's® Plastic Coating on an object that is subsequently kept in the dark, a reaction takes place that causes them both to yellow very quickly. However, if the object is then put in a light place, this discoloration eventually lessens.

Sylmasta®

Like Milliput®, Sylmasta® is an epoxy putty consisting of two parts, which you mix in equal amounts. The hardener is buff coloured and the resin white; when combined they form an off-white mixture. Because Sylmasta® is a little softer than Milliput® it is easier to blend and allows a slightly longer working time (if this is a consideration). It can be smoothed using water, acetone or talc. Although it starts to go off in about one and a half to two hours, it takes another one and a half before it begins to harden properly. Because of this, it may need extra support while curing. It cures fully in twenty-four hours and sets harder than Milliput®.

All three of the putties described above are very useful for hard modelling replacement areas *(see pp. 78–9)*, such as arms of figures, teapot spouts and so on, as they can be shaped easily before curing and worked, once cured, with files or other suitable tools.

Polyesters (car body/marine fillers)

These, perhaps surprisingly, are another type of material suitable for filling porcelain. There are several of these fillers on the market, all of which have similar properties. They come in the form of a paste to which you add 3 per cent hardener. It is not essential to be absolutely accurate in the measuring, though it is probably better to be too sparing rather than too generous with the hardener – too much will prevent the mixture from curing properly.

The great advantage of using these polyester pastes lies in the speed at which they enable you to fill an object – they set in minutes, much quicker than any epoxy – although the short setting time does reduce the size of the area that you can fill with any one mix. In addition, they can be smoothed with acetone shortly after mixing, and can be cut back easily with a scalpel before they reach full cure. However, because they are mixed as a paste, they are not suitable as a modelling material.

Plastic Padding®

This is a two-part polyester paste, which should take about ten to fifteen minutes to harden at normal room temperature. It is advisable to fill large gaps with a number of separate mixes, as this filler shrinks while curing. The smaller the area filled with each mix, the less overall shrinkage there will be.

Plastic Padding® has a thin consistency when first mixed, which allows you to fill small holes. Another advantage it has is that when you feel it beginning to 'pull' at your spatula, you know you have about a minute before it becomes impossible to work the resin. Plastic Padding® rubs down easily, takes paint well and is a good filler for a beginner. It is not, however, ideal for use on white porcelain, because it is grey in colour.

David's® Isopon P 38

This also consists of two parts: resin and hardener. Although it is similar to Plastic Padding®, there are certain differences:

- Its colour is a brownish off-white.
- It does not seem to shrink if used in small amounts at a time.
- It sets very suddenly, after about four to five minutes at room temperature.
- Small holes do occasionally occur during rubbing down.

The first two properties give it an advantage over Plastic Padding®, which, however, scores higher on points three and four.

Marine® Filler

This resin is a very light grey; unfortunately the hardener, which is yellow, turns the cured resin pale green. To get a whiter mix, it is possible to use a different brand of hardener. I use a white-to-opaque hardener from a grey polyester resin called Sebralit®; mixing it with the resin of Marine® Filler produces a really white paste. The hardener can be purchased from the Sebralit® supplier without the resin. (Sebralit® resin is not ideal as a filler for porcelain because it sets extremely hard and is thus difficult to rub down). Using a different brand of hardener does not seem to have any detrimental effect on the Marine® Filler. It is workable for about five minutes, during which time it will gradually thicken and become more difficult to spread smoothly, until it begins to drag against the spatula. It sets in about ten minutes at room temperature and shrinks only very slightly whilst curing. I like this product and when I need an opaque filler, i.e. one that will need painting, this is the one I use.

F.E.W.®

This has the same properties as the other polyester fillers but scores over them in its colour, which is almost white, and in its ease of application. It also rubs down to the most superbly flat, smooth finish, perfect for painting. Use small amounts at a time because it begins to go off in about three minutes and is fully cured in about fifteen. Like Marine® Filler, it gets thicker as it sets and drags against the spatula creating a roughness on the surface. Many of my restorers really like this filler, but for me it is a little too soft to work with. I would recommend that you form your own opinion.

Regardless of which filler you choose, the method of use is the same. The length of time you will have in which to complete the operation, however, will vary according to the curing time of the filler you are using. With experience you will know just how much to mix at a time, so as to avoid unnecessary wastage.

Gap filling

When filling a gap, you need to push your chosen material firmly against the backing to achieve as smooth and flat a fill as possible on the back as well as the front, so it is vital to make sure that you have secured this backing properly.

For gap filling you will need

- Backing or support material.
- Sellotape®, masking tape or Magic® tape.
- A hot-air blower (such as a hair dryer) or hot water easily accessible (if you are using wax as the backing material).
- Acetone and talc for smoothing.
- White tissues or cotton wool.
- Filling materials.
- A small piece of glass or a tile.
- A metal spatula.
- Greaseproof paper.
- Wooden cocktail sticks.
- A scalpel to remove any excess filler.
- Abrasive papers.
- Support for the object, such as a cork ring or a sand box.

Procedure for gap filling

Once you have assembled your tools, examine the area to be filled and select the section of original porcelain that corresponds most closely to your missing part. Then consider from which face the impression needs to be taken. If raised decoration has to be incorporated, take your impression from the face on which this decoration appears. If this is not a consideration, take the impression from the less accessible side and introduce the filler, which will need much more work on its unbacked surface in the way of smoothing and finishing, from the face that is easier to reach. For example, the inside of a vase may be difficult to get at, so the backing material should be pressed on to the inside and the filling material introduced from the outside. Similarly, if you are filling a hole in the bottom of a bowl, you should place the backing material on the inside and fill from the outside.

For the purposes of the following description, the assumption is that you are working with a sheet of dental wax.

Hints and tips

Beware of 'trapping out' (*see pp. 48–51*). If, for example, you want to take an impression of an overhanging rim or lip, do not extend the backing too far or you will not be able to remove it without distortion; you may then have to cut it away from the overhang. If your object has such a feature, a silicone rubber putty may be a better choice of backing material because of its flexibility (*see pp. 90–1*).

1 Take your wax and cut it slightly larger than the gap you wish to fill, leaving an overlap of about 1cm (about ⅓in) all around. If the missing area is very large, you can melt two or more sheets and join them together. In this case, however, you will probably have to provide additional support to prevent the wax from sagging when you introduce the filler. A suitable support material for this purpose is X-lite®, an open-cell bandage of polyester mixed with an inorganic filler, which you shape by heating. Gently warm the wax, either by using a hot-air blower or by leaving it in warm-to-hot water until it softens slightly. If you use water to soften the wax, dry it thoroughly with tissue before proceeding; it is very important to remove all traces of water, as the moisture may inhibit the curing of some fillers. Once it is soft, place the wax quickly on to an identical but undamaged area of the vessel, to achieve the correct shape. For the edge of a plate, such as the one illustrated here, you will need to fold the wax over the rim. Using your fingers, push the wax hard against the porcelain until the colour of the porcelain shows evenly through it. A foggy appearance indicates that you have not pressed firmly enough; keep working the wax until you are satisfied, then allow it to harden before carefully removing it.

2 Take a tissue dampened with acetone and run it down the broken edges to remove any dirt or grease. Place the shaped wax over the missing area, then take a piece of tape and with it fix one edge of the wax to the porcelain, to hold the backing in place while you adjust it. It is very rare for the backing to match the contour of the missing area exactly, so take your hot-air blower and gently heat the wax around the edges, checking the fit front and back.

3 Applying a little pressure, push the edges of the wax against the surface surrounding the missing area until it fits perfectly. Be careful not to press too hard or the wax may intrude into the space you are about to fill. Accuracy at this stage can save you a great deal of work when sanding down. Once you are satisfied with the positioning, fix more tape to the porcelain along the remaining edges of the wax. You are now ready to start filling.

4 If you are using a polyester filler, take your piece of glass or tile and cover it with greaseproof paper. Tape the paper down firmly, for it is on this that you will mix your filler. Mix it as recommended by the manufacturer, paying careful attention to quantities. If you are using an epoxy putty you may find it more convenient to knead the two components together with your fingers (wearing gloves). Now take some filler on your metal spatula and press it against the edge of the porcelain. It is very important to achieve a good contact between the filler and the porcelain edges. Work in this way till all the broken edges are covered.

5 Now start to fill the hole left in the centre, taking care not to disturb the wax backing. When it is filled to the correct depth, take the flat face of the spatula and stroke it across the surface to smooth it, lightly placing your other hand behind the wax to give extra support, if possible. During this process you must be aware of the shape you are trying to match. Try to ensure before the resin cures that the contour conforms with that of the original. If the level of the filler dips slightly, keep adding more until the surface is flush with that of the porcelain. If, however, you have overfilled, you have time to remove the excess with a scalpel before the filler fully cures (remember, though, that you will have less working time with the polyester than with the epoxy fillers). It is better to underfill initially, and then to add more filler as necessary, rather than apply too much and then have to file or carve away the excess. Overfilling is, in fact, one of the commonest mistakes beginners make. It is, however, something they soon put right once they discover how time-consuming it is to sand down a raised, fully cured fill.

6 At this juncture, the surface of the filler is likely to look a little bumpy. If it does, take your smoothing material (acetone or talc) and smooth the surface – without losing the shape you have achieved. You can apply the talc with a tissue using small, circular motions with a little pressure to flatten the bumps. Another method, and the one I prefer, is to apply the talc with your fingers to achieve the same effect. If you use acetone, apply it on a cotton wool swab, but take care not to flood the surface during the process. For polyester, talc will be effective only if used immediately after the filler has gone off; acetone, however, can be used easily for up to an hour and a half, and if you apply pressure you can achieve some effect with it even after the surface is completely hard. When the filler appears reasonably level leave it to harden. When it has cured remove the wax backing. At this stage you can fill any holes in the surface with the same material.

7 The final stage of filling a gap is sanding. It is quite effective to wrap your sanding paper around a pad of Plastazote®, which gives a firm, flat surface to work with. For fine filling of very small holes it is preferable to use one of the following products, which are especially made for the purpose.

Materials for fine filling

Fine Surface Polyfilla®

This is a smooth paste that comes ready mixed in tubs or tubes and is obtainable from any hardware shop. Use a small spatula to push the filler into the holes, leaving it a little proud, then allow it to dry for about an hour before rubbing down. This filler gives a very smooth finish and takes paint well.

Cellulose stopper

This filler is available from car repair and accessory shops. It is a thin, premixed paste that you apply with a small spatula and it sets hard in about five to ten minutes. It can, therefore, be smoothed much sooner than Fine Surface Polyfilla®. Though softer than some other fillers, it gives such a good finish that some restorers give the whole of the restored area a coat of stopper (smoothing it down) before applying paint. As cellulose stopper sets by the loss of a solvent, continually opening the tin causes it to become thicker and thicker, until it eventually becomes unusable. You can thin it down with cellulose thinners but it is best to avoid the problem by always replacing the lid immediately after use.

ABOVE Fine filling with Modostuc® followed by further light rubbing down prepares the restored area for painting.

Modostuc®

This is an Italian-made fine surface filler. Although it is not widely available outside Italy, you can order it direct from the manufacturers. It is a very smooth paste that dries quickly; it also dries slightly softer than Fine Surface Polyfilla® and is, therefore, easier to rub down, giving a very smooth surface for painting (*see left*).

The above three fillers are liable to shrink (although Modostuc® does not shrink as much as the other two), so do not use them to fill large holes.

Colour-matched fillers

Hxtal® NYL-1, Araldite® 2020, Fynebond® and Epo-tek® 301 are water-white epoxy resins that have already been described under 'Adhesives' (*see pp. 55–7*). You can, however, also use them as fillers by adding colorants together with thickening agents, such as fumed silica, to achieve a perfect match with the colour of the body and/or glaze of the piece under repair. They are ideal for translucent porcelain because you can control the degree of opacity (as you cannot with denser fillers) according to how much bulking agent you add. When this method can be made to work it is probably the best one to use, but it is very difficult to master. I have known some of my colleagues to produce a fill of an identical colour to that of the original body or glaze, but my attempts merely result in one that is adequate in texture, contour and finish but has to be painted in the same way as the traditional fillers in order to achieve an exact match. Why, then, should you spend time trying to perfect the process? There are three good reasons:

• Compared with any of the false glazes available at present, these resins take far longer to discolour.
• You can fill the missing area precisely, whereas when you are spraying over a fill that needs painting it is impossible to avoid overlapping some of the original surface (unless you have masked it off first).
• Although the resins are expensive, you do not have to bear the cost of purchasing an airbrush and a compressor.

Fumed silica (such as Aerosil® R805 or Cab-O-sil® M5) added to the resin will act as a thickening agent. The resin will lose its transparency slightly but will remain translucent; the more you add, the less translucent, as well as stiffer, it will become. If you are making a thick paste, it is not likely to escape from the backing; however, if your filler is semi-viscous it could still seep out, so you must be absolutely sure that the backing material is tightly fixed to the porcelain body in order to prevent any leakage occurring.

Procedure for using colour-matched fillers

1 Measure out and mix on a watch glass the required quantity of your chosen resin in its recommended proportions, then add the fumed silica, a little at a time, blending it in thoroughly with a spatula until you achieve the consistency you require. If you need a fairly stiff paste but want the resin to remain translucent, add less fumed silica and leave the mixture to cure slightly before use.

2 Take small quantities of the mixed paste and thoroughly incorporate a little of each of the colours you may need, building up a 'palette' around the edge of the glass. Add small amounts of these mixed colours to the resin and silica paste to achieve a match with the body, glaze or decoration. There are many different brands of the various paint mediums available and it is up to you to find the one that suits you best. Dry ground pigments and Maimeri® Restoration Colours are both very good. Of the two, I find the Maimeri® colours easier to use, as they mix very easily with the resin, whereas pigments take longer to blend in (for *further details on colours, see pp. 103–106*).

3 Apply the mixed, colour-matched resin using a spatula or a cocktail stick (*see p.106*). Depending on how thick you have made your paste, it will need to be either pushed into the missing area to achieve good contact with the edges or just applied and then left to find its own level. Add more as necessary to bring the fill flush with the original surface. If you are using a thinner mix, the object needs to be carefully balanced or supported so that the resin does not run out.

Cork rings can be extremely useful for this purpose, especially as they can be cut easily to size and shape in order to support awkward-shaped objects.

There are other effective ways of working with coloured fillers. One is to make a thicker paste to use as a core to simulate the body and then to sandwich this, once cured, with a semi-viscous, possibly tinted, layer on both faces to simulate the glaze. In order for this technique to succeed you must make sure that the backing material fits snugly into the gap (rather than covering and adhering to the outer surface of the porcelain), and that it corresponds exactly with the depth of the original glaze. Secure it firmly with tape so that you can press the paste in without dislodging it. Fill only to the thickness of the core, leaving space for the glaze coat to be applied. The glaze coat on the other face will occupy the space left once the backing is removed. You may want to match the thick paste to the colour of the body, particularly if the surface layer needs to be translucent. If, however, you need a dense colour for the glaze layers you may not have to colour the body fill at all. Where greater opacity is needed, micro-balloons will produce a better result than fumed silica. For a completely opaque core, polyester paste is probably your best option. Leave it to cure before applying the epoxy glaze layer. An advantage of using polyester for the core is that it is considerably cheaper than the specialized epoxies; for this reason it is the best option if you have a large area to fill and a budget to consider.

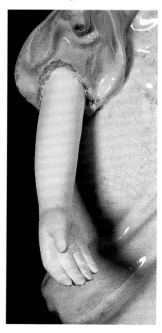

BELOW The replacement arm on this *blanc-de-Chine* figure has been made slightly thinner than the original, allowing space for the application of a specialized epoxy resin to simulate the glaze.

This method of making a core and covering it with a simulated resin glaze is also ideal for replacement arms of figures (*see left*). Model the arm in an epoxy putty such as Milliput®, making it slightly thinner than the original, and leave it to cure. Then make up the glaze to a gel viscous enough to coat the core to the thickness of the original and to stay in position while it cures. If the job is skilfully done, no finishing should be necessary.

If the piece you are restoring has underglaze decoration with the blurred outlines so often found on oriental blue and white you can successfully simulate the effect either by applying the white resin immediately after the blue, so that they merge with each other, or by gouging the pattern out of the cured white resin and substituting blue resin. Leave this to cure, sand the surface, and you will create a fuzzy edge. You can then apply a clear glaze.

Finally, specialized epoxy coloured and used as a gel is ideal for replacing missing enamels on ceramics or metalwork. Mixed to the right consistency it will sit proud of the surface and perfectly match the original.

With colour-matched fills it is essential to mix enough resin to replace the whole of the missing area in one operation, because of the difficulty of achieving exactly the same colour a second time. It may be prudent to mix a little more than you think you will need and place any leftover resin in the freezer compartment of a refrigerator so that it will remain usable for a further one to four days (depending on which resin you are using) in case you need to add to or redo any areas.

Once the resin has cured it may be shaped by softening slightly with acetone if necessary, then cutting back the excess with a scalpel or sanding, as with other fillers. If the cured resin turns out to be the wrong shade after all, you can scrape away the surface layer with a scalpel and replace it with a new batch of a more accurate colour. Whereas other fillers would have to be painted, these, if you have achieved a perfect colour match, need no more than a polish to give the effect of a glaze. Use finer and finer grades of Micro-mesh® cloth (*see p. 78*) and perhaps a polishing cream (*see p. 143*). If you are not happy with your colour and despair of achieving a satisfactory result using this method you can always paint and/or spray over what you have done and then finish as above.

An alternative to cutting back or sanding a coloured fill is to place a piece of clingfilm or Melinex® firmly over the resin while it cures. It is easy to remove, and you will leave a very smooth surface that may not need any further work.

Where a very high gloss is needed, you can paint on a clear coat of resin as a glaze; this, too, may need smoothing and polishing to achieve a perfect finish.

Break filling

This type of fill is sometimes necessary when two fragments stuck together have chipped edges or small holes along the line of the join. These holes and chips are sometimes virtually invisible at this stage, but if you are going to spray or paint along your joins it is essential to eliminate them for a layer of paint will show up even the smallest blemishes. The problem is less likely to occur if you have used a specialized epoxy for sticking, as it will probably have run into the chips and filled them automatically. If not, you can add more along the join line and cut it back, if necessary, once it has cured.

The main difficulty in filling tiny holes when using conventional epoxy putties or polyester pastes lies in the fact that these fillers are too thick to give a really smooth finish. In these circumstances it is best to use a small amount of one of the premixed fine fillers, such as Fine Surface Polyfilla®. Push the filler along the line of the join, applying pressure as you go: the flat end of a small metal spatula is perfect for this task. For individual deep holes, push the filler into the hole, using the hook end of the spatula, exerting some pressure if necessary (rather like a dentist filling a tooth). Leave the filler to harden, and then sand it.

Sanding materials

There are many different types of abrasive paper, all easily obtainable from hardware stores. Glass papers, garnet papers and silicon carbide papers (all of which come in various grades) are the most suitable for use on fillers that require painting; your choice of grade will depend on how successful you have been in achieving a smooth finish at the filling stage, but whichever you start with, you will need to work your way through to the very finest ones. It is up to you to decide which type you prefer. Silicon carbide has the advantage of being suitable for both wet and dry use – wet giving the smoothest finish of all.

> **Warning**
> Putting resins into a refrigerator used for food contravenes health and safety regulations.

It is best to use the abrasive papers in small pieces, rolled up or wrapped around a little block of Plastazote®. The most important thing is to avoid the original porcelain while you are sanding, as it can easily be scratched.

If you have used a specialized epoxy for your restoration, abrasive papers will be far too coarse to use for finishing; you will need a finer material such as Micro-mesh®. This is a flexible, abrasive cloth, obtainable from specialist suppliers in coarse, medium and fine categories, with three grades in each. One grade from each should be sufficient. It comes in sheets, rolls or flexi-files, and has the further advantage of being washable and reusable. In fact, Micro-mesh® is an extremely good fine finisher for all types of filler, not just the specialized epoxies, and because it is a cloth it is particularly useful for sanding awkward areas that abrasive papers would be too stiff to allow you to reach.

Modelling

When an object has lost an arm, leg, head or handle the restoration process becomes much more difficult. Two quite distinct techniques using largely different materials are employed to replace this type of missing part: the first is modelling, the second moulding and casting (*see p. 81*)

I must stress from the outset that I am not, and probably never will be, an expert modeller. In my experience few people are capable of direct modelling – taking a piece of modelling material and being able to produce a near-perfect replica. Some, like myself, can at least manage to 'carve' the desired shape from a roughly modelled form. Others are capable of neither modelling nor carving, but rely on taking a mould from a similar piece or area.

There are two methods of modelling a replacement part: hard and soft modelling. In the former, the modelling medium acts as the replacement material and is ultimately fixed to the object. The latter technique is used as a preliminary to moulding and casting, and in my opinion is best reserved for really difficult cases, such as a figure with a missing head or for a very finely detailed piece, where you might need a longer working time to achieve a good result. You would also choose this method if you needed to cast a fairly translucent part with a specialized epoxy. Which method you use is for you to decide.

Hard modelling

This process involves the use of a resin or putty, which, after mixing, you apply directly to the missing area (taking care not to overfill along the junction line), model as far as possible into the intended shape and leave to harden. After curing, you can, if necessary, define the form more precisely by carving with a scalpel, shaping with needle files (which come in a whole range of shapes: flat, half-moon, round, triangular and so on) and sanding with abrasive papers. The extent of the modelling you do before the material cures will depend largely on

how expert a modeller you are and, of course, on the curing speed of the resin you have chosen. A disadvantage of this technique is that the modelled area can sometimes sag during the hardening process, although the chances of this happening vary, depending on the sort of missing part you are trying to replace as well as on the initial softness of your chosen resin and/or the amount of bulking agent you have added. The problem can be overcome by supporting the appendage with a suitable material, such as plasticine; alternatively you can try 'wire modelling'.

At least three of the epoxy resins/putties are suitable for hard modelling – Araldite® 2011 (originally 2001) with white pigment and a bulking agent such as kaolin added, Milliput® and Sylmasta® (*see pp. 67–8*). Of these, Sylmasta® tends to be the most elastic and, thus, the most likely to sag while curing; on the positive side, its softness makes it easier to shape and sand. Araldite® is more adaptable because you can adjust the level of bulking agent to give a stiffer or softer mix as required. Milliput® is a popular hard-modelling material because it holds its shape well.

As all three are epoxies, the bond between the resin and the porcelain is generally good. If there is any slight movement at the point of junction you will need to remove the added piece once it has cured and restick it using an epoxy adhesive, but always ensure that the sticking area is free from grease or dirt or the bond will not be firm and discoloration may become a problem.

Wire modelling

You can overcome the problem of sagging in modelled replacement arms, legs, handles and so on by using a non-corroding wire support (*see right*). In principle, this is a good idea; however, the old method of attaching the wire by inserting it into a hole drilled into the porcelain risks damaging the object and, thus, cannot be recommended. I prefer to cut the wire to length, shape it and then stick it to the broken edge of the porcelain with a large blob of epoxy adhesive. Once the wire is in place you can cover it with putty or resin, according to preference, and then model and finish it as described above. The wire may come unstuck while you are working, but I feel that the nuisance of resticking it is preferable to the danger of the drilling process. If you feel you must use the drilling method (bear in mind, however, that diamond-tipped drills are not cheap) be sure to work with the tip of the drill under water to avoid overheating.

Soft modelling

Soft modelling, as its name suggests, involves the use of a soft, non-curing material. Its advantage over hard modelling is that the material will stay pliable, giving you as much time as you need to produce your replacement piece. From this, however, you will then need to take a mould. You can either attach the modelling medium directly to the missing area and shape it, or shape it away

ABOVE An arm on a porcelain figure is modelled in stages using a wire support.

from the object, perhaps on a board or an upright post. If you use this latter method, you will need at some late stage in the modelling to press your piece into place on the porcelain at the point of junction between the two, in order to achieve a good fit. Once it is finished, carefully remove the piece and mould it away from the object prior to casting. It is a good idea to put a separating layer, such as clingfilm, between the porcelain and the modelling material in order to prevent it from sticking and making the porcelain greasy.

Several modelling materials are suitable for this process; four are described below. Wet clay is also possible, although it does tend to shrink.

Block wax
This is of a harder consistency than the other suitable materials and, therefore, tends to hold its shape better. You can shape it using scalpels and wooden modelling tools, but for a really smooth finish it is best to use a heated spatula.

Plasticine
For years I used plasticine for all my soft modelling, preferring it to block wax because it was so easy to work and smooth down. Although I tend to use block wax for most of my modelling nowadays, I still find plasticine much more convenient for replacing larger areas. It has the disadvantage of drying rather hard at room temperature and has to be kneaded to soften it enough for modelling, but once soft it can be worked with any of the usual modelling tools and easily smoothed with water. It does, however, tend to be greasy, so if you are modelling directly on to the object, you should protect the broken edge with a separator, such as clingfilm. Always choose white plasticine, as coloured types may stain the porcelain or moulding material.

Newplast®
This material, which is similar to plasticine, comes in strips of various colours, though it is best to choose white for porcelain restoration. It has the advantage over plasticine of staying soft at room temperature. It holds its shape better than plasticine (though not as well as block wax) and is easily smoothed with water. It is not greasy, but you would probably be wise to cover the broken edges with clingfilm to protect them from the grease on your fingers.

Plastiline®
This product, though also known as 'French modelling wax', is very similar in appearance to plasticine. It is available in ivory or grey in three consistencies: very soft, medium and very hard. I find the medium consistency most suitable because it holds its shape and yet is soft enough to work easily. It comes in a block and appears quite hard, but when portions are broken off they can be softened very easily by kneading. It is finer than either plasticine or Newplast®, however, so although it retains its shape well, once you have modelled it you

should avoid handling it more than you need, for the warmth from your fingers could soften it and distort the piece you have created. If you need it to be very soft, wrap it in polythene and hold it under hot water for a short time; repeated heating will, however, cause it to lose some of its plasticity. If you want it to harden more quickly, put it in the refrigerator. The manufacturers suggest using methylated spirit to smooth it, but water works perfectly well. Although it is not greasy, you should still protect the broken edges with clingfilm.

Finishing

The finish of any modelled piece must be as smooth as the surface of the porcelain. A good finish is easily achieved with soft modelling because you have unlimited time to work the surface. With hard modelling, two main faults are commonly found in a 'finished' piece: a bumpy surface, in clear contrast to the line of the original, and an obvious junction between the original and the modelled part. Both of these faults can be overcome during final sanding. Your new piece will have been worked (unless you are a very fine modeller) with needle files prior to this finishing stage, so you must check to see if you have left any striations on the surface. If so, these must be smoothed with fine-grade abrasive papers.

When you have completed your model and are satisfied with the finish, you are ready to proceed with either painting (if you have chosen hard modelling) or moulding and casting (if you have soft modelled).

Moulding and casting

Moulding is perhaps the most useful skill in the repertoire of any restorer, as it can save hours of painstaking work modelling – provided, of course, that you have a piece corresponding to the missing area from which to take the mould. If not, you have no option other than to model the missing piece first.

It is necessary to define from the outset the two very distinct processes of moulding and casting. Moulding is taking an impression of an area, using a material that can be removed, which will then contain the negatively shaped space of the piece that has been moulded. Casting is the process of filling this empty space with a material that will harden to produce an exact replica of the original. It is essential for the moulding material to be compatible with the casting material (*see p. 92*).

Moulding

We have already discussed the simplest form of moulding – the open wax mould used as a backing material for fillers (*see pp. 71–3*). The following section describes how to make a straightforward one-piece mould in latex (*see pp. 83–6*) and, for more complex objects, correspondingly complex moulds of two or more pieces in silicone rubber (*see pp. 87–90*).

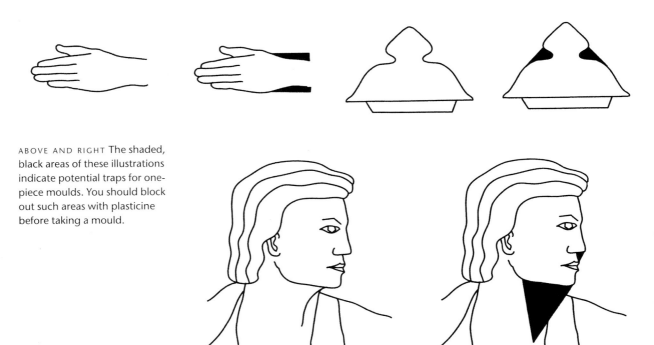

ABOVE AND RIGHT The shaded, black areas of these illustrations indicate potential traps for one-piece moulds. You should block out such areas with plasticine before taking a mould.

In the past, restorers who wished to mould an object had no option other than to use plaster of Paris. Though it is still in use today, this material sets rigid and demands a great deal of expertise if you want to make even the simplest mould without the risk of damaging the porcelain. I would certainly not advise anybody who is not an expert to attempt to mould plaster of Paris directly on to porcelain because it is so easy to 'trap' the porcelain into the plaster. If this happens, then the plaster is quite likely to break when you attempt to remove the mould. Worse still, you could even break the porcelain.

Fortunately, there is no longer any need to run this risk, for today you have a choice of flexible materials available that allow you to mould quite deep undercuts without any fear of being unable to remove the mould cleanly after it has set. Plaster of Paris is still widely used as a casting medium (*see pp. 92–4*), but as a moulding material on porcelain it is employed nowadays only to create a strengthening outer casing for flexible moulds – such a casing is termed a 'mother mould' (*see p. 90*). Even when making semi-flexible moulds, though, you may still have to use a blocking-out material, such as plasticine, to reduce the likelihood of a trap (*see above*).

There are at present three excellent materials that are used by virtually all porcelain restorers for the making of flexible moulds. These are latex, silicone rubber and silicone putty.

Latex

This is a thin, liquid rubber with a small amount of ammonia added. The type most commonly used by porcelain restorers is dipping latex, although many other varieties have been developed. For years, latex has been the most popular material for making moulds because it is easy to use and relatively cheap, is flexible, takes a good impression and, when bulking agents are added, is very strong. In fact, too much bulking agent will turn a latex mould almost rigid. There are, however, some disadvantages with this material: the mould will not keep for any length of time (it shrinks within months), so casts are normally taken within a few weeks of moulding; it can also become distorted, though bulking agents may help to minimize this problem. If there is any gilding on the object you are moulding, the ammonia in the latex could damage it, so you should test it with a small drop of latex in an inconspicuous place. To be completely safe, it may be better to use a separating layer of tinfoil, clingfilm or Whatman® laboratory film before moulding, provided that there is not too much raised detail on the surface.

ABOVE Moulds were taken of the spout and handle of the seventeenth- or eighteenth-century Qing dynasty *blanc-de-Chine* hexagonal wine ewer on the left, in order to restore the damaged example on the right.

Making a one-piece latex mould

For a simple one-piece mould, such as the one taken from the teapot spout illustrated here (*see above*), which was then used to replace the missing spout on a similar teapot, the procedure is as follows:

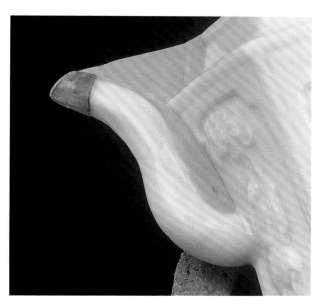

1 First block off with plasticine any pierced areas (in this case the spout hole), plus any areas that are likely to cause traps (it is also possible to make a one-piece mould of an object with slight undercuts if you first block these out with plasticine). Apply the latex thinly over the area to be moulded, using a cotton wool bud on a stick, or an old paintbrush. You may need two or three coats and then a final, thicker, reinforced layer. Always cover a larger area of the object than you actually need, for the edges of the mould can be rather ragged and often have to be cut off. Dab the first coat on to the surface of the porcelain – never paint it – taking care not to go over the same area twice, for as the latex touches the surface it begins to set and if you disturb this process you will spoil the mould.

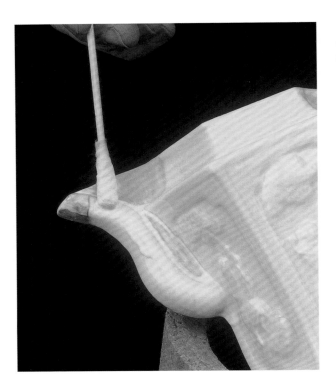

2 The latex will be white when first applied but as it dries it will become colourless to light brown depending on the thickness of the layers.

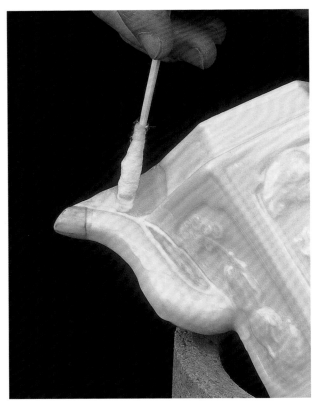

3 As the first coat begins to dry and change colour, after about fifteen minutes, apply another. The timing of the application of this second coat is important; it must not be too soon, or the first coat will be disturbed, nor too late, or the two coats will not fuse properly together. The first coat must, therefore, be firm but still a little tacky. The second coat has to be dabbed on like the first and then allowed to dry. A third layer may be applied in the same way if required.

Hints and tips

Once you have applied the latex you can heat it if you like under a desk lamp, to shorten the setting time. The porcelain should be turned occasionally to ensure that the cure is as even as possible. If you use heat, however, remember that the process creates stresses in the mould that cause it to deteriorate and lose its shape more quickly; in these circumstances you will need to use it as soon as possible.

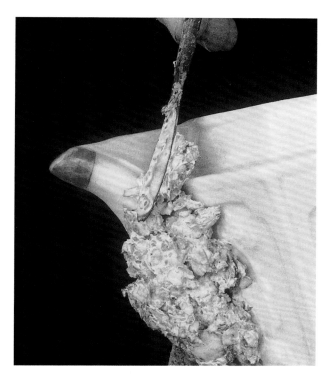

4 You should now apply the final coat, again at the slightly tacky stage to ensure good adhesion. Depending on how flexible you want the mould to be, this coat may contain a bulking material that will strengthen the top layer and thus the whole mould, helping to keep it in shape. Take care not to apply too thick a coat or you will find it difficult to remove the mould from the porcelain. Suitable bulking agents are gauze, fibreglass matting, vermiculite (as shown here) or sawdust. When using gauze or fibreglass, first cut it into suitably sized strips and then dip these into the latex, ensuring that they are completely saturated. Apply them to the surface, taking care not to disturb the underlayers, overlapping each strip of bandage with the next to ensure that the whole area is covered.

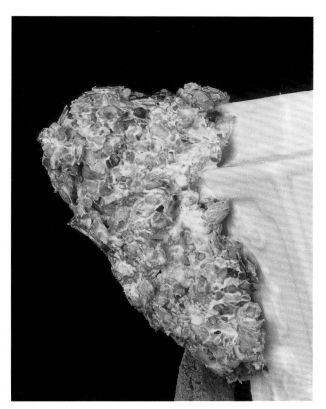

5 Then apply a second layer in the opposite direction to the first and allow both to dry naturally. If you are using sawdust or fine vermiculite, mix it directly into the latex to make a paste and apply it with a spatula. Be careful not to add too much, for if the mix is too dry it will not form a good bond with the layer underneath. The thickness of the top layer will vary from object to object, but for most moulds 1.25cm (½in) is thick enough. Allow this layer to dry naturally. As well as providing extra strength it will prevent tearing – particularly helpful if you are making a large mould or if the mould is to be used more than once.

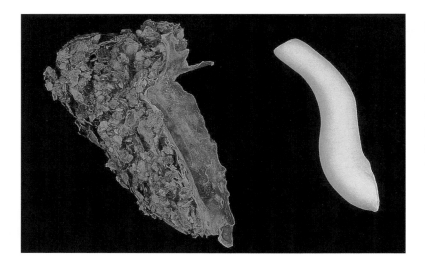

6 When the latex has completely cured, after about twenty-four hours, remove the mould from the porcelain and dust the inner surfaces with talc to prevent them from sticking together. The negatively shaped space of the mould is now ready to cast from. Here you can see the mould of the spout, together with the plaster cast that was taken from it.

Silicone moulding materials

Silicone rubber products are by far the best moulding materials currently available, having all the qualities necessary for the purpose: they take a perfect mould when used correctly, they are reasonably strong and, unlike latex, they will not shrink. When these materials were first produced they really were made from rubber; today, however, they consist mainly of petrochemical components, though they are still known as 'rubber'.

In comparison with latex, silicone rubbers are very expensive (though silicone putty, which is much quicker to use than either silicone rubber or latex, is at least cost-effective in terms of time saved). Because of the cost involved, there is not much point in using them except for moulding intricately detailed pieces, or for moulds that you wish to keep for some time. For straightforward, 'no detail' moulding, latex works perfectly well and is considerably cheaper.

Silicone rubber

There are many silicone rubber products on the market made by a variety of manufacturers, though some are more suitable for restorers than others. I have selected two for discussion.

Elite® Double

This consists of two semi-liquid parts: a pink base A, and a clear activator B. These have to be mixed in a ratio of 1:1 by weight to form a bright pink, semi-viscous gel. You can pour this immediately over the surface of your object; if, however, you are moulding something – an arm, for example – around which you cannot build a retaining wall (*see pp. 87–90*), it is advisable to wait for about four to six minutes until the gel becomes viscous enough to apply without risk of it dripping. It begins to set in thirty minutes at room temperature. Once cured, it is soft and flexible and so can be removed easily; for this reason it is ideal for objects with slight undercuts. You can use the mould more than once, although with repeated use it will begin to tear.

Some coloured moulding materials can stain the resin cast; with Elite® Double, however, the colour remains stable after the first cast with epoxy resin. Although subsequent casting causes lightening of the mould area that comes in contact with the resin, which would normally suggest that the colour has run, the clear epoxy cast does not show signs of any colour contamination. It would seem that the resin causes a chemical reaction in the silicone rubber, rather than the other way around.

Silcoset® 105

This product also comes in two parts: the rubber itself, which is white and very runny, and a catalyst. It is mixed in a ratio of 100 parts rubber to 1 part catalyst by weight, which works out as 10g (about ⅓oz) of resin to three drops of curing agent. It begins to go off after about five hours but takes up to eight hours to reach full cure. You can also buy a rapid-curing agent, but remember that this will shorten your working time. It also tends to make the mould more brittle.

The technique you use will depend on what you want to mould. For something with a level base, such as a lid, you can just pour on the rubber mixture, but you will first need to construct some form of enclosing wall of a suitable material, such as plasticine – Silcoset® is so runny that without this barrier it would simply flow all over the place. To be absolutely sure of avoiding air bubbles you could dab the first coat on with a paintbrush or a cotton wool bud and then allow this coat to set before pouring on the rest of the mixture. Indeed, if the part to be moulded is one that cannot be laid flat – the arm of a figurine, for example – it is essential to dab on the first layer in this fashion, not only to ensure a good contact but also to minimize the risk of dripping. Allow the mixture to cure completely, and then incorporate into the next layer a bulking agent, such as fumed silica, adding enough to form a paste so thick that it will cling to the object. If you follow this procedure you will be able to manage without actually having to construct a plasticine wall.

Making a complex silicone rubber mould

Silicone rubber is a perfect medium for complex objects that require a mould of two pieces or more, such as the example on the following pages. As a first step, block in any pierced areas with plasticine. Then use more plasticine to make a dividing wall along the desired join line of the two halves of the mould – for example, down the centre of the handle, inside and out, pressing it firmly to the porcelain with the hook end of a spatula to prevent the moulding material from leaking under it. Make the face of the wall on the side to be moulded as smooth as possible. On the other side, strengthen it, if necessary, with balls of plasticine at any weak points.

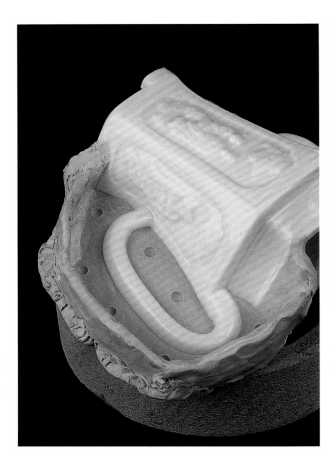

Hints and tips

At the outset, decide if you will need to make an air outlet for the casting medium. When moulding directly from an object, such as the wine ewer shown here, you will produce a mould with an open end that should be wide enough to allow air bubbles to escape if you pour your casting material carefully down one side. If, however, the opening is very narrow, you will need to make an air outlet hole before starting. For an enclosed mould (one made away from the object) you will need to have two holes – one for pouring in and one to allow the air to escape. The object you are moulding and the material you are using to make the casting will determine how big the access holes should be. If you are using one of the specialized epoxies, you need only a very narrow access hole and outlet. Cut lengths of drinking straw and press them through the plasticine wall at the two highest points of the object, so that one end touches the porcelain and the other projects beyond the wall. Keep the straws in place during the moulding and casting processes.

1 You now need to make a keying system to lock the two halves of your mould together. You can do this either by making a series of indentations in the plasticine or by pressing a length of fuse wire or other suitable material into it, following the line of the shape to be moulded. Before making the first half of your two-piece mould, support your object in a suitable position and build up a retaining perimeter wall of plasticine around the area to be moulded, attaching it to the smoothed dividing wall.

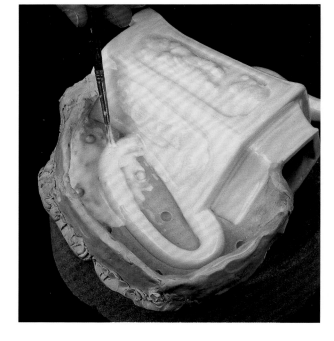

2 If you wish, first apply with a brush a thin layer of silicone rubber both to the object and to the smoothed inner face of the plasticine.

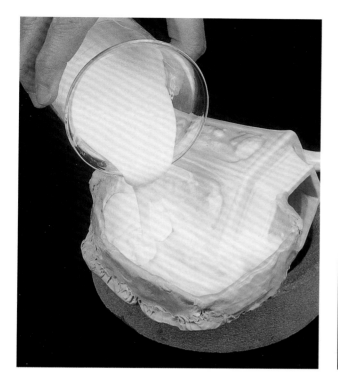

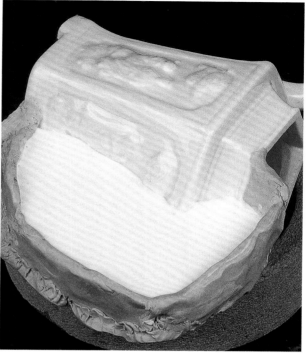

3 Let this dry and then pour more silicone rubber over the area until it is completely covered. When the rubber has set (after about 8 hours), remove both plasticine walls, leaving the first half of your mould in position. If you have used fuse wire for your keying system, remove it at this stage.

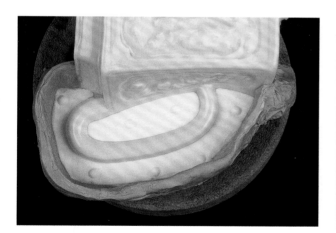

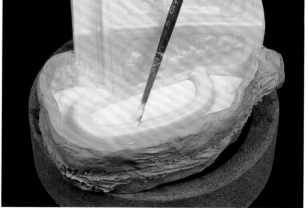

4 Now turn the object over and build another plasticine retaining wall around the other half of the piece to be moulded.

5 Coat the exposed surface of the section you have just moulded with a release agent, such as talc or Vaseline®, and then apply a thin layer of rubber directly to it.

6 When the rubber is dry, pour in more until the area is completely covered. Once the rubber has set, the mould should be easy to remove. As a test, whenever you make a mould, and after it has dried, hold it up to the light and carefully inspect your handiwork. This inspection will show you immediately if there are any thin areas that you need to reinforce with more moulding material.

Mother mould

Very large moulds require a 'mother mould'. Such a mould casing is normally necessary when the area to be moulded is so large that the final layer containing the filler would have to be of an unmanageable thickness, or when the weight of the casting material would be such that it would change the shape of the mould or cause it to twist. A mother mould is made, before the latex or silicone is removed from the porcelain, by covering the moulding material with a thick layer of plaster of Paris. There are certain things to consider before applying the mother mould:

• Will the shape of the inner mould allow you to remove it easily?
• You need to make it in the same way as the original so that the sections of the inner and outer moulds correspond.
• Always give the inner mould and each section of the mother mould a good coating of Vaseline® as a release agent.
• Never make the mother mould too thick – it is better for it to break than not to come off at all. If you are in any doubt, make the mother mould in more than two pieces.

Silicone putty

This is a very effective moulding material, taking a sharply defined impression of even the smallest detail. It is used in medicine to take impressions of the ear in the making of deaf aids, and of teeth for dentures (and is thus completely non-toxic), and in recent years has been adopted increasingly by porcelain restorers to make small moulds. One of its biggest advantages is that it takes a very short time to cure – usually between five and ten minutes. On the down side, this short curing time makes it unsuitable for use on very complex, three-dimensional objects or for making large moulds. The cost of making larger ones would probably be prohibitive in any case, as these putties are very expensive when compared with latex (though I am not taking into account the cost of labour when making the latex mould). The number of brands available has increased dramatically, with almost all the big manufacturers now producing at least one type. Indeed, the choice has become so wide as to be confusing, and new ones, I feel sure, will continue to come on to the market. I have selected just two examples for comparison.

Provil® novo

This comes in regular or fast set, but the fast-set type does not really allow you enough working time – about one minute – before it begins to go off. I advise you to choose the regular set. This consists of a turquoise-coloured base and a white catalyst (both putties) that you mix in equal amounts by kneading them together into a soft impression material. It takes about thirty seconds to mix the components to the required degree: their contrasting colours make it easy to see when they are thoroughly blended. At room temperature you have only two to three minutes' working time before the mix begins to go off, and it will be completely set within seven minutes. The putty takes an excellent impression and is quite flexible, thus allowing you to mould fairly deep undercuts.

Optosil®

This consists of a white putty base with a red liquid catalyst. It is mixed in a ratio of 8–10 drops of catalyst – which is equivalent to about 16g (½oz) – to one level measure of putty (a scoop is provided). You can mix the two components together in about thirty seconds. At room temperature, you have about three to four minutes' working time, and the putty will set completely in about eight minutes. If it is not mixed thoroughly, Optosil® has a tendency to layer. Like Provil®, it takes an excellent impression and, being even more flexible, can be used for very deep undercuts.

After mixing, you use both putties in the same way. Using your fingers, press the putty over the area to be moulded to ensure good contact with the surface, making sure that it does not become too thin. As a rule, the thickness should be no less than 5mm (⅛in) and no more than 20mm (¾in), depending on the extent of the area to be moulded. When the putty has gone off, remove it by pulling it from the surface by one corner. All the casting materials may be used with the silicone putties.

Casting

When you have made your mould, you can begin the casting process. I would suggest that your first cast should be what is termed a 'plaster master'. This is a cast taken from the mould using plaster of Paris. Once the cast is dry, seal it with a lacquer, such as shellac, and then store it away in case a similar shape is wanted in the future. A plaster master collection can save much time and effort; especially useful items include handles, lids, arms and legs.

A casting material must have the following characteristics:
- It must be liquid enough to run into the mould and displace all the air in it.
- It must be small-grained enough to take up the finest detail of the porcelain.
- It must be strong enough to take a few knocks without breaking, or else be able to accommodate a strengthening material.
- It must be workable once set. Casts often come out with faults, flash lines and so on, and removing these can be laborious if the casting material is too hard.

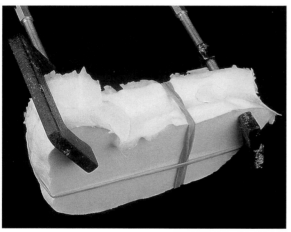

BELOW The two pieces of a mould may need to be clamped together or secured with elastic bands while the plaster cast cures.

There are several materials available that meet these requirements. Your choice of casting medium depends on what you are casting and the final effect you want to achieve – whether or not the cast has to be translucent, for example. Cost may be another factor.

The three main types of casting material used by restorers are plaster of Paris, epoxy resin and polyester resin. Before taking a cast you need to coat your mould with a release agent to prevent the casting material from sticking to it. You can buy special agents for use with silicone rubbers, but Vaseline® or talc should suffice. Secure the sections of the prepared mould with clamps or elastic bands to ensure an airtight join (*see left*).

Plaster of Paris

Although used for centuries as a casting material, plaster of Paris still has its place today. It is cheap, easy to work if left for twenty-four hours, and good at picking up detail on pieces that are not too complicated. (If the detail is very fine, air bubbles may become trapped and form pinholes on the surface of the cast). Plaster is available in various grades and strengths and comes in the form of a powder, which you add to cold water.

Superfine casting plaster

I have tried many types of plaster of Paris over the years, but now tend to use superfine casting plaster, as it has a very fine grain and is reasonably strong, yet does not set so hard that it is difficult to carve or sand.

Crystacal® R; dental casting plaster
These products are popular choices. Crystacal® is brittle
and very dense, but does give you twenty minutes'
working time before it goes off; dental plaster will begin
to harden after five minutes.

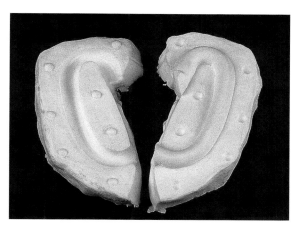

ABOVE The two-piece mould
opposite, with its clamps and
bands removed, open and
showing a cast handle.

Procedure for plaster casting

1 Sprinkle the plaster on to the surface of the water and
allow it to sink. Gradually add more until it begins to
show just below the surface of the water, then let it stand
for about one minute (to give the water time to permeate
the plaster) before stirring.

2 Stir slowly, to avoid incorporating air into the mixture, and thoroughly, to
disperse the powder and prevent lumps from forming.

3 Tap the side of the container to release trapped air, which will rise to the
surface in the form of bubbles.

4 When ready, the mixed plaster should have the consistency of double cream.
It will begin to thicken very quickly, so you should pour it into the mould
without delay.

5 When pouring plaster (or any other casting material) into a mould, if you
have not made a pouring hole with an air outlet, pour steadily from one place,
letting the medium slowly fill the mould and push out the air as it occupies the
empty space. A small mould, like the one of the handle shown above, should be
ready to open after about two to three hours. Leave larger moulds overnight.

6 When you remove the pieces of a complex mould, you will probably see flash
lines along the junctions of the sections. These can be fettled off with a scalpel
(*see right*).

BELOW Carefully fettling the
flash line on a plaster cast
handle using a scalpel.

Consolidating a plaster cast

In its natural state, plaster is too fragile for most
porcelain restoration jobs, so if you use it, some form
of strengthening will be necessary. The easiest method is
to soak the plaster cast in a consolidant for two to three
hours – you will probably see lots of air bubbles rising
from it – or you can apply the consolidant repeatedly
with a paintbrush until it is fully absorbed. The best
consolidants to use are Frigilene® and Ercalene®,
which are ready-made lacquers for metalwork. As an

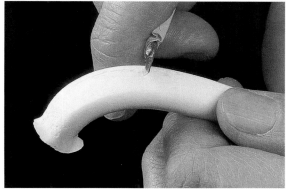

Warning
When you are making up consolidants you should use a fume cupboard or wear a mask.

alternative, Paraloid® B72 mixed to a 5–10 per cent solution in 50/50 acetone and IMS works well.

The following recipe also makes an effective consolidant: take a tube of HMG®, empty it into a container and add about twice as much, by volume, of acetone. When you remove your plaster cast, wipe the consolidant from it immediately with an acetone-soaked tissue to prevent a build-up of resin on the surface, and leave it to dry. The results can be most satisfactory, and plaster that has been consolidated in this way can even be used in place of the harder casting materials. An alternative method of strengthening the cast is to add PVA emulsion to the plaster mixture in a ratio of about one teaspoon to a cupful of plaster. Although it will never be as hard or durable as the hard resins, even after consolidation, plaster is ideal for quick casts and masters.

Epoxy Resin

Araldite® AY 103/HY 956

This resin (*see p. 54*), which is still available only through specialist outlets, is much more fluid than the mass-market Araldite® adhesives we are accustomed to using. It is mixed in a ratio of approximately 5 parts resin to 1 part hardener by volume. Its curing can be delayed or even prevented by high humidity levels, especially if a large surface area is exposed. In such conditions, you should cover the resin once it is mixed, and leave it to stand until curing is under way before starting to use it. A short resting period is desirable regardless of atmospheric conditions, as it gives the air bubbles time to disperse. At room temperature you have a working time of three and a half hours and the resin reaches full cure in twenty-four hours. Because of the heat generated when large amounts of the two components are combined, the manufacturers recommend that amounts less than 250g (8½oz) only are mixed at a time. (You are unlikely to need as much as this anyway.) As the AY 103 is almost clear, any detail in the moulding will not show up well unless you have added a bulking agent, such as kaolin, which will give a degree of opacity, and/or a white pigment, such as zinc oxide or titanium dioxide. Unfortunately, neither can simply be added directly to the resin and stirred, as pockets of unmixed powder will be created, which will come to the surface while the resin is curing and form holes in the cast. You can prevent this problem from occurring by taking about one tablespoon of the mixed resin and incorporating into it a similar amount of the powdered bulking agent and a small amount of pigment, if required, until you have a smooth paste. Then mix this paste into the main body of the resin. Repeat the process until the resin is as thick as double cream. Pour the mixture into the mould and leave it to harden; it will be fully cured in twenty-four hours.

Hxtal® NYL-1, Araldite® 2020, Fynebond® and Epo-tek® 301

If you want to create a translucent or very fine fill, these specialized epoxies are ideal. Because they are so runny, they are also the best for enclosed moulds with narrow access holes. Mix them as described in Chapter 4. You may also add fumed silica (but not so much that the mixture becomes too thick to pour into the mould) and colouring agent, if required. Specialized epoxies are, of course, very expensive, particularly if you are using them in the larger quantities that are often needed for casting.

Polyester resins

Trylon EM 306PA and EM 400PA

There are various polyester resins available on the market, including EM 306PA and EM 400PA, but these products are not as good for casting as the epoxies. Their advantage lies in the fact that they are very cheap. This type of resin has a separate catalyst, which you have to mix in. The proportions vary from brand to brand, so make sure that you read the manufacturers' instructions. Once mixed, the resin begins to give off a certain amount of heat, so as a precaution never mix it in a flimsy yogurt pot or margarine tub; instead use a tough polythene container.

These resins are sold under a variety of different names, the most common term for them being 'casting resin' or 'embedding resin'. Trylon makes a range of very good colours (*see p. 106*) especially for mixing with polyester resin, should you wish to colour-match to your porcelain body. The resin will be fully cured in twenty-four hours, although any surface exposed to the atmosphere will remain slightly sticky, thus ensuring a good bond in cases where you have to apply several layers. Even if you cover the surface with tinfoil or Melinex® while the resin is curing, it may remain slightly tacky; in which case you may need to sand it gently.

Polyester resins have other drawbacks in addition to those mentioned above. Often, on mixing, the resin suffers badly from air bubbles, so it is advisable to allow the mixture to stand for a while in order to give the bubbles a chance to disperse before pouring it into a mould. When the cast is removed from the mould it is very hard and, therefore, difficult to work. You should not use large amounts of this material to fill a latex mould; there is an incompatibility between the polyester and the latex, and heat generated by the hardening resin could possibly cause it to stick to the mould. (This problem does not arise with silicone rubber or silicone putty moulds.) Araldite® AY 103 is always preferable to polyester resin but unfortunately it is not easy to obtain, whereas the polyester resin is more readily available.

The extent to which a cast will need finishing will depend on the quality of your mould, whether or not it has flash lines and so on. Place the cast in position on the object to see how well it fits. If there is any excess resin, you can remove it with a small fret-saw and/or files – but take care to cut as close to the lines of the original as possible. If there are any flaws on the surface or along the flash lines, they can be disguised with a fine surface filler. Once you are satisfied, stick the cast to the object using an epoxy adhesive.

Warning
Polyester resins give off toxic fumes and should never be used in an enclosed area; use extraction and a mask, or at least ensure that you have as much ventilation as possible.

Spinning

A problem all too often encountered by the porcelain restorer is that of the missing lid. Many beautiful teapots, bowls and boxes are brought into the workshop without their lids, and their owners ask you to make new ones. This is unlikely to be a straightforward task. To begin with, you will probably need to do some research to determine the most suitable design. If you can find a lid of comparable style the best option is to make a two-piece mould from it, especially if it has complex raised detail. If you can only find an illustration of something suitable, you can still model your own version and cast from it.

In general, however, the best way of making lids or replacements for large missing areas of pots and so on is to 'spin' them. The ideal method is to use a potter's wheel with a jollying arm attached, to which you can secure a template; the arm can be easily raised or lowered as required. If, like most people, you do not have access to a potter's wheel, you can make a very simple spinning machine yourself or commission a local workshop to make one for you.

The spinning machine in its simplest form consists of a wooden frame of two upright bars secured with brackets either side of a wooden base plate at least 15cm (6in) square and joined by three horizontal crossbars of equal thickness, one above the other (*see below left*). A metal rod with a flattened lower end containing two bolt holes passes vertically through aligned holes in the horizontal bars, exactly above the centre of the board. You attach the template to the end of the rod by pushing the two V-shaped cut-outs on to the bolts, which you then tighten so that template and rod rotate freely together.

This arrangement works well for small objects but because of the lack of rigidity in the sheet metal of the template, a degree of distortion tends to occur in the spinning of larger shapes (unless you stick a wooden former to the template to make it more rigid). Here, the solution is to secure the template top and bottom with horizontal bars so that it cannot move, and to spin the clay instead by means of a banding wheel (*see below right*). The central rod is

RIGHT This is the simplest form of spinning machine. The template is turned on a central rod. The inset detail shows how the template is secured with nuts and bolts.

FAR RIGHT Here the spinning wheel can be seen with a template secured over a banding wheel.

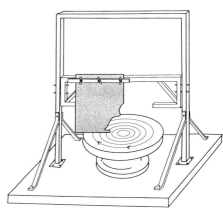

dispensed with; instead you bolt the top edge of the template into place on a wooden or metal crossbar by means of wing nuts through drilled holes; you must position the inner edge of the template directly over the centre of the wheel. A further supporting bar and bolts projecting from one of the uprights and fixed near the bottom of the template ensures complete rigidity. You can enlarge the wheel by adding a circular piece of wood to enable larger pots to be spun. Locking bolts fixing the crossbeams to the uprights allow you to raise or lower the bar to the desired height. The design of these machines, and the materials from which they are constructed, may of course be adapted to suit individual requirements.

The template

As you will have to make the template yourself, first you will need to decide which material to use. I have tried various options, including wood, hardboard and perspex, but I always return to sheet metal (1mm gauge) because in my opinion the sharpness of its cutting edge makes it by far the best material for the purpose. The piece of metal sheet should be large enough to allow room all around after the required shape has been cut from it to ensure that it can be firmly attached and will remain strong when in use.

Procedure for making a template

If you have a similar example from which to make a template for your missing piece, and have access to a template-maker, you will be able to save yourself a lot of time and effort. A template-maker is a device consisting of numerous paper-thin, movable brass rods which, when pressed against the side of a curved object, adapt themselves to its outer shape, or profile. The rods can then be fixed by screws at either end. Once you have taken the profile of the pot, place the template-maker on a sheet of tracing paper, using a central vertical line as a guide, and draw the required shape. You will have to gauge the thickness of the pot using callipers before drawing the inside profile. Use an adjustable clamp-stand and ruler to measure the exact position of any external features, such as a lip or handles, which you will have to add after you have spun the object.

To make a template in cases where you have no existing object to work from – for example, for a replacement lid (*see above right*) – proceed as follows.

First, draw two lines at right angles on a piece of tracing paper (*see p. 98*); the vertical line **a** will represent the central axis of the lid. Ascertain the diameter by measuring across the flange of the ewer and halve it to find the radius, then mark this distance on the horizontal axis **b**. After deciding on the shape and height of the lid, mark the height on line **a**, then draw a line **c** freehand between the two marks on lines **a** and **b**. This will be the outside shape of the lid. Establish the thickness you require (it may be helpful to note the thickness of the ewer rim) then draw a line **d** to represent the inside shape of the lid. Turn

ABOVE This seventeenth-century blue and white ewer is typical of the kind of piece that may be presented by its owner with a request that its missing lid be replaced.

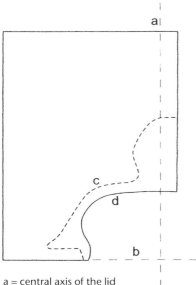

a = central axis of the lid
b = horizontal axis
c = outer profile of lid
d = inner profile of lid

the tracing paper over and, using a soft pencil, draw over the shape on the reverse, then transfer the drawing to the metal and tape it in place so that it cannot move. (Ensure that your template has a straight bottom edge with which to align the paper.)

Now trace the drawing on to the metal through the paper, including the line **a**, as this is required to line the template up with the centre of the wheel. Remove the paper and cut the inside shape out of the metal along line **d** using tin snips. If you are using a central rod, you will need to leave enough extra metal to the right of line **a** to allow the two v-shapes to be cut so that they align with the bolts that will secure the template to the spinning machine. You may need to file the cutting edge of the template to make it completely smooth.

Using the template to spin a lid

Although spinning is essentially a simple process, you may find it useful, especially if you are not using an electric wheel, to have an assistant to help you by removing excess clay from the template and making sure the plaster is mixed at the right stage. Sharing the workload will ensure that the job runs smoothly (*see opposite*).

1 Attach the template of the missing lid to the jollying arm, as shown here, if you are using a potter's wheel, or to the frame of your spinning machine. It is very important to get the bottom edge of the template level with the wheel base plate – if it is not exactly parallel, the lid you spin will be misshapen.

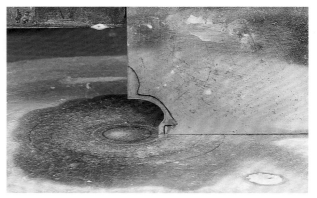

2 As a guide, draw a series of concentric circles on the base plate using a pair of compasses – a potter's wheel head will probably already have a series of grooves cut into it. Dampen the wheel head with a little water and then attach an appropriately sized ball of soft, grey modelling clay very firmly to the centre, adding more clay if needed a little at a time until you have built it up to the right height.

3 Now turn the wheel (or template if you are using the simpler machine) and the template will begin to cut the clay into shape. Be careful not to apply more clay than you need, or the resistance may cause the template to bend and distort.

4 As the shape begins to emerge, remove the excess clay with a spatula. Your finished shape must be as smooth and free from holes as possible because any defects will be transferred to the plaster lid you are about to spin.

5 Before removing the template, it is essential to mark its exact position so that you can be sure to refix it in the same place. Cut the outside shape –
line **c** of the template shown opposite – and file the edge smooth. Now fix the template back in position: the space between the template and the clay should correspond to the shape and thickness of the required lid. It is essential for the space to be uniform all the way around, which it will not be if you have not replaced the template exactly in its original position.

6 For the first layer, mix enough plaster to cover the whole of the clay shape. Pour it over the clay, starting at the top, spinning the wheel at the same time (or pulling the template around the clay former in the case of a fixed machine). Be careful not to let too much plaster accumulate on the template or allow dried particles of plaster to remain on its edge – they will mark the lid's smooth surface. Therefore, finish spinning each coat before the plaster starts to dry: it should be creamy while you are spinning or you will begin to damage your surface. While the first coat is drying, mix more plaster for the second. Dampen the first layer to prevent too much absorption of water from the second layer – you do not want this to dry out too quickly.

7 Apply the second coat in the same way as you did the first; it should begin to fill any holes that were left in the surface. You can apply a third, thin layer of plaster as soon as the second layer of plaster has gone off; this should give you a very smooth finish. The whole process needs to be done quickly.

RIGHT The new plaster lid in position on the ewer, before painting.

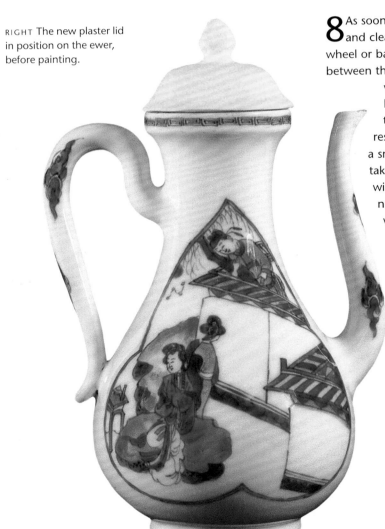

8 As soon as the job is finished, remove the template and clean it. Scrape off any excess plaster from the wheel or base plate with a spatula. Pass a cheese wire between the spun lid (still with its clay core) and the wheel or base board, so that you can easily lift the lid free once it has hardened. Leave the plaster lid on the machine overnight. If it resists removal the following day, simply push a small spatula under it. You can then carefully take out the clay core, and you will be left with a plaster lid, which can be smoothed if necessary, but should require very little in the way of further work. You can either use this lid as it is (consolidated with two or three coats of lacquer) or take a mould from it and cast it in resin. Once dry, it is ready to be sprayed and painted. The finished unpainted lid is shown here, united with its ewer (*see left*).

Colour mixing

6

Many people feel that false glazing and painting are the most important parts of the restoration process. My view is that no one element of the job is more important than another, for they are all inextricably linked: a bad join will always look bad even when it is beautifully painted; holes in fills can be disguised to some extent but they will still be visible. For these reasons you should not start to mix your colour until you are completely satisfied with the surface to be painted.

False glazing resins

For some years now restorers have been using synthetic resins both as a vehicle for paint and to simulate glazes; nowadays, however, we are much more aware than we used to be of how dangerous they can be to the user. I cannot stress this point often enough: before using resins and their thinners it is essential to ensure that you use some form of protection against the fumes they produce. Fume extraction is the ideal solution; if this is not possible, wear an appropriate mask.

Leaving aside the health and safety aspects, a resin, if it is to be suitable for false glazing, should have the following important properties:

- It should not damage the original porcelain.
- It should be easy to remove, even after several years.
- It should be mixable with a colour without altering that colour's properties and appearance.
- It should set hard enough to resist being marked by a fingernail.
- It should adhere firmly to the filling material.
- It should be water-white and remain so for a reasonable length of time (at least ten years).

Even among the recently developed resins I don't think there is any one that gives restorers exactly what they need, though we are a little closer than in the past. It is the problem of discoloration that remains unresolved. The only resin that combines colour stability with the required properties of hardness and gloss (Torlife® Clear Polyurethane Resin) is, unfortunately, not safe to use without extremely efficient fume extraction. The resin market is constantly changing, however, and I am confident that before long restorers will be presented with a product that meets all their requirements. The following resins, which cure either by the addition of a catalyst or by the evaporation of a solvent, are among the most effective currently available.

Urea formaldehyde

Rustin's® plastic coating

This product is available in clear, white or black and cures by the addition of a catalyst in a ratio of 4 parts resin to 1 part hardener, measured by volume. It sets to a hard, durable surface in twenty-four hours at room temperature and hardens to a gloss finish in two to three days.

The formula of Rustin's® changed a few years ago and it now takes much longer to discolour, especially if it is kept in the light. Rustin's® thinners can be used both to thin the paint/resin mix as required (especially when spraying) and to clean brushes and airbrushes. Most colouring mediums will easily mix into this resin.

Epoxy

Sylmasta®Cold Glaze Two-part System

You can obtain this product in either a clear or a white base; it is also available in three types of finish – gloss, satin or matt. Sylmasta® cures with the aid of a catalyst and you mix it in a ratio of 2 parts resin to 1 part hardener, measured by volume. It sets to touch dry in about two to three hours, hardens in twenty-four hours if kept at room temperature and will produce a tough and durable finish in seven days. Under scientific testing, it was slower to discolour than Rustin's®. You can use Sylmasta® thinners in the same way as Rustin's® thinners, both to thin the paint/resin mix and as a brush/airbrush cleaner.

Acrylic

Daler-Rowney®, Winsor & Newton®, Liquitex®, Golden®, Paraloid® B67, B99

All of these brands of acrylic resin set by loss of a solvent. Although you can use them as an alternative to the Rustin's® and Sylmasta® products described above, they do not set as hard; with the exception of the Daler-Rowney® acrylic gloss, they are probably too soft to simulate a porcelain glaze. Paraloid® B67 and B99, which can be made up with an appropriate solvent, have good colour stability and are next in hardness to Daler-Rowney®, though they may be more difficult to obtain.

Water-based

Golden® Porcelain Restoration Glaze

Golden® has recently produced a water-based, fast-drying, false-glaze medium. It is obtainable in either a gloss or a matt finish and both produce a tough and durable surface when fully hardened. In common with all the other resins, it can be sprayed or painted on and can be sanded between coats. All the Golden® paint products can be mixed into it but if you are intending to spray you should use Golden® Airbrush Colors, which have been designed specifically for use with an airbrush.

Colouring mediums

There are many different materials to choose from when it comes to colouring false-glazing resins, the most widely used being dry ground pigments, varnish colours (Maimeri® Restoration Colours), acrylic colours, coloured polyester pastes and coloured epoxy pastes. You can obtain most of these products in an extensive range of colours, and some are also available in light, medium or deep shades. Their degree of transparency is governed by the amount of colour you add to the resin. Some colours are weaker than others, however, so that no matter how much you add you will not achieve a really strong tint with them. You will learn by experience which ones best suit your purpose. Although it would be desirable to have the full range of colours, it is not absolutely necessary. The following list comprises a good cross-section:

(NB: The pigments below marked with an X are toxic)

Cobalt blue	Cadmium orange	Indian red
Winsor blue	Chrome orange (**X**)	Alizarin crimson
Prussian blue	Raw sienna	Cadmium red
Manganese blue (**X**)	Yellow ochre	Vermilion (**X**)
Cerulean blue	Lemon yellow	Raw umber
Cobalt green	Chrome yellow (**X**)	Burnt umber
Chromium oxide (**X**)	Light red	Titanium white
Viridian	Burnt sienna	Lamp black
Winsor green	Venetian red	

Pigments

Pigments are derived from a wide variety of sources; many are of mineral or plant origin, although nowadays increasing numbers are synthetically produced. Most of the major paint manufacturers produce pigments and they vary in two important ways: first, in the coarseness of the pigment and, second, in the price you have to pay for them. Over the years I have used a number of different makes, ranging from the coarse, water-based pigments to the finest-ground, dry ones. There are two good reasons for using pigments: the range of colours is wider than you will find in any of the other mediums and they are also compatible with and mix easily into all the resins used for false glazes. I have a great affection for pigments because the depth of colour that can be achieved with them is just right for porcelain restoration.

Winsor & Newton®, Kremer®, Maimeri®
Among the best pigments are those manufactured by the art material giant Winsor & Newton®. The range of colours you can purchase from this company is vast and, on the whole, reasonably priced, considering that a 30-ml jar of

pigment will last for years. Kremer® pigments are very finely ground and come in an even wider colour range, but they are slightly more expensive. Maimeri® also produce, in addition to their varnish colours, a good colour range of very finely ground pigments with comparable prices. Within each range the cost of individual colours varies greatly, however, depending on their source and on whether they are organically or synthetically produced, so it is wise to think carefully about the shades you are likely to need in your particular field of work, rather than spend a lot of money buying a complete set.

Finely ground pigment mixed into a resin produces a paint containing very few visible particles, thus reducing the risk of marring the surface of your restoration. You can further reduce this risk by grinding the pigment even more finely with a spatula as you add it to the resin, a task that I consider essential. Some pigments grind down better than others; there are a few that are of no use to the porcelain restorer – *terre verte*, for example – because they are so resistant to grinding that they form dots of undissolved colour in the paint layer.

Varnish colours

This colouring medium contains gum of Chios and turpentine in place of oil and has largely supplanted the oil paints that used to be so popular.

Maimeri® Restoration Colours

In most respects Maimeri® colours are very similar to oils. They come in 20ml tubes and are available in a wide range of colours (though not as wide as that of pigments). The thick paste has a strong covering power and mixes very easily with the resin. They can also be used straight from the tube but would then need to be sealed with a coat of resin once dry. They are ideal for spraying because they do not need to be ground before use. Maimeri® colours are fairly expensive to buy but they will last a long time, as a little goes a long way. It is important to keep the thread on the screw tops of the tubes free of paint, however – if the threads become clogged, the lids will not fit properly and the contents will dry out.

Acrylic colours

The base of this paint medium consists of acrylic resin rather than oil. There are many companies supplying acrylics in an extensive range of colours. They can be opaque, transparent or translucent (the variety will be indicated on the pot or tube) and they can be used straight from the tube or mixed with water if necessary to obtain the exact shade you require. They can be brushed or sprayed on, forming a layer of paint that dries quickly to a matt-like appearance. You can then paint the pattern on by hand, and spray on a final resin layer as a glaze. As airbrushes were originally designed for use with watercolour, acrylic colours thinned with water are ideal if you want to avoid the risk of clogging your airbrush nozzle with a thicker resin, such as epoxy.

I have used this method only a few times on porcelain; because acrylics on their own are not as hard as a resin and pigment combination, I usually reserve them for use on pottery. However, most big companies have now introduced colourless acrylic mediums, with a choice of gloss or matt finish; mixing the colours into these produces a harder and stronger finish. I have two reservations about using acrylic colours: first, they do tend to dry to a darker shade; and, second, I am not sure that the adhesion between the paint and the restored area is strong enough. Acrylics tend to dry out rather easily, so it is important to keep the thread of the screw top and neck of the tube or jar free of paint and replace the lid immediately after use.

Daler-Rowney® Cryla Artists' Acrylic Colours

These are widely available from art suppliers and come in 38ml or 120ml metal tubes. The paint is fairly thick and if you apply it by brush straight from the tube your brush strokes will be visible on the surface. If, however, you thin it with water, it dries to a flat, smooth finish with good coverage.

Liquitex® Acrylic Colours

Liquitex® colours come in plastic 59ml and 138ml tubes with a screw-top cap that is bigger and somewhat easier to handle than the cap on Daler-Rowney® tubes; they are also available in jars of various sizes. The paint in the tubes is only slightly thinner in consistency than Daler-Rowney®, and your brush strokes will still be prominent unless you thin the paint with water – if you do this, coverage should be smooth and even.

The paint in the jars is much thinner than that in tubes, and you can obtain a very flat, smooth surface by applying the paint straight from the jar. You can also achieve a more opaque finish with the paint from the jars compared with that from tubes because you need less water to reach the same consistency. Its fluid consistency makes it ideal for spraying, mixed 50/50 with water. It dries slightly more matt than the tube paint.

Golden® Artist Acrylic Colors

These are available in 119ml plastic pots with a wide, screw-top lid that makes it easy for you to remove just the amount you require. There is a good colour range available and the colours come in a variety of finishes. Golden® Fluid Acrylics are of a medium consistency; although they do not appear very different from the tubed Daler-Rowney® and Liquitex® brands, they paint to a very flat surface straight from the pots, with no brush marks. When mixed with water they give an extremely even, smooth coverage. They also have very high pigment levels and, therefore, retain their colour strength even when mixed with a medium. Golden® Heavy Bodied Acrylics are deliberately designed to be of a very thick consistency. Mixing them with water or other mediums will give you a smooth, flat surface but will, unfortunately, also dilute the colour

ABOVE Coloured specialized epoxy being applied with a cocktail stick.

strength. Golden® Matte Acrylics are very similar to the Heavy Bodied types, but they have a matting agent added. Golden® also produces a range of airbrush paints, which are available in opaque or transparent finishes. Transparent types have 10 per cent of the strength of the opaque colours. They both provide good colour intensity. Airbrush colours are of a much thinner consistency and the particles will separate out if left standing. The manufacturer advises that the jars should be shaken every day in order to prevent pigments that have settled at the bottom from clogging. If this procedure is not followed the heavier particles will become impossible to mix with the rest of the paint and the overall colour will be affected as a result.

Polyester paste
Trylon
This is a good product that mixes very well with the appropriate-based resin. The range of colours available is relatively small, however, when compared with that of pigments or acrylics, although translucent colours are also available. Polyester paste comes in small jars, so it is easy to extract the precise quantity you require. The colour intensity is very strong, so you need to use only a tiny amount in order to obtain the desired shade.

Epoxy paste
Araldit®-Farbpaste
These colours, which come in tubes, are recommended by the manufacturer to be used in the proportions of 4cm paste to 1g resin, but they are extremely strong, so you need to be extra careful about the amount you add to your resin. Do not automatically follow the directions but proceed even more cautiously than with other colouring mediums, adding a very small amount of paste at a time to the resin until you have achieved the exact shade you want.

Colour matching

The art of colour matching is, unfortunately, a skill that cannot be completely taught. The restorer has to have sufficient visual acuity to be able to look into a colour and discern how it is made up. For example, you can buy white resin, but I have never restored a piece of 'white' porcelain on to which I have been able to spray this white and achieve an immediate match. To the porcelain restorer there is no such colour as white; all the whites of porcelain have some colour to them, a colour that is unique to a particular piece. It is often tempting, if you are restoring a number of cups and saucers from the same tea service, to mix up one base colour for them all. This practice cannot be recommended, as there are likely to be very subtle differences of shade between individual pieces, which you may not notice until you are actually applying the paint.

For white porcelain, in particular, the overall appearance of the glaze is also an important factor: if it is clear, has it a predominantly bluish or greenish hue? Occasionally, a clear glaze will be so thin that its inherent colour will be difficult, if not impossible, to discern. If this is the case, you should look at the places where the glaze has a tendency to build up – for example, around the foot ring, the junction of handles or any depressions in the surface of the porcelain. These thicker areas emit the true colour of the apparently clear glaze.

ABOVE Testing a mixed colour against a colour-matching square outlined in masking tape. (Private collection)

It is impossible to give recipes for colours; restorers have to create their own according to their individual needs. There are, however, certain steps that you can take to help you to decide on the correct shade. If you are not experienced in using paints it would be a good idea to experiment with your colours on paper before attempting to use them on porcelain; find out how dense or transparent you can make each one, how they mix together and how wide a range of shades you can achieve. Light plays a vital role in colour matching, as it does in the examination of broken edges, so always mix colours in daylight (preferably bright but indirect light), never under ordinary fluorescent light, unless you know that the piece is to be displayed under such lighting. If the destination of the object is uncertain, mix your colours near a window under a daylight lamp. It is possible to purchase light bulbs or tubes that are specially made for colour matching (Philips® have a good range); they emit a bluish colour that is close to daylight. However, don't be fooled by tubes called 'daylight' – they never entirely live up to their description.

The colours in a pattern can be very distracting when you are trying to mix a base coat, for any light reflected from the pattern into the glaze can mislead you into mixing the wrong shade, particularly if you are working on a highly decorated object. Even if the colours from the pattern are not being reflected into the glaze, their very presence can deceive. To overcome the problem, make a colour-matching square the size of a postage stamp, with the aid of masking tape (*see above right*). The tape prevents you from seeing anything outside the colour you are hoping to match.

For spraying or painting you will need

- A fume-extraction unit or a mask.
- Your chosen colour medium and resin.
- Appropriate thinners.
- A sheet of clear, thick glass, approximately 15cm (6in) square, on which to mix your paint.
- A small-to-medium spatula or palette knife, to blend the colouring medium into the resin. Such an implement is essential if you are using pigment colours, as they need to be thoroughly crushed before use. The flat blade of the spatula ensures that you obtain a good, even mixture.
- An airbrush and accessories.
- Good-quality paintbrushes.
- White tissues.

Mixing colours for spraying or painting

It pays to be methodical and meticulous in your colour-mixing procedure; clean your mixing surface and tools frequently and set out your colours in a neat row. Clear glass makes an ideal mixing surface; the thicker the glass the better, as it adds nothing to the colour being mixed. I find that my eyes focus at the level of the glass and not on the colour of the bench beneath it. An alternative to this, and a method used by many restorers, is to mix your paint on a pure white tile. I suggest you try both methods and see which you prefer.

1 Clean your glass with acetone, making sure that you remove all traces of dust, dirt and any previous mix of paint. Then clean the spatula. Choose the colours you think you will need and line them up close to your mixing glass.

2 If you are using a catalyst-curing resin do not add the catalyst until you are satisfied with the colour you have mixed, because the setting process starts immediately. (If you are inexperienced, it could take you quite a while to achieve your colour match.) Although setting can be postponed by adding thinners, thinned resins tend to be softer than unthinned ones.

3 Carefully measure the required amount of resin and hardener but keep them in separate containers at this stage. Along the top half of the mixing glass place a little of each of the colours you have chosen. If you are using pigments, you will need to crush them thoroughly, using the flat blade of your spatula, before incorporating them into the resin. It is a good idea to mix each of your colours into a very small amount of unmixed resin to make a paste – remembering to clean the spatula thoroughly between colours – before beginning to build the shade that you require by mixing into the remaining unmixed resin in the container a little of the paste from each colour as necessary, checking all the time either by eye or by direct comparison with your colour-matching square.

When I first started restoring and my eyesight was keener, I could match colours simply by looking back and forth between the mixing glass and the object; I could easily see what needed to be added in order to achieve the correct shade. Nowadays, I have to compare the two by applying the mixed colour directly to the porcelain (which is probably the method that works best in any case). If, for example, you are mixing a white base, place

Hints and tips

There are four important things to remember when mixing colour for your porcelain repair:

• Start with the light colours and then add the darker ones; it is always easier to darken a colour than to lighten a dark shade.

• Some colours when added to others will change their original hue: for example, if you have a yellow-tinted white that is too bright and you need to tone it down, do not add black or you will end up with a muddy green. In general, it is wise to steer clear of black if you are trying to darken a colour: raw umber is more likely to give you the shade you are after.

• If you want to lighten a colour, adding a tiny amount of lemon yellow is far better than using white, which may well deaden the colour if you add too much.

• Until you gain more experience, colour matching is very much a matter of trial and error, so allow yourself plenty of time to get it right.

a small blob of the paint/resin mixture on the corner of your colour-matching square with a paintbrush; make sure the blob is fairly thick, for a thin film will not cover adequately and the true colour of the porcelain will show through and affect your judgement. Consider the difference between the two. Is the white too strong? Is the porcelain a yellower or a bluer white than your mixed colour? What does your white lack? Go through your range of colours and select the ones you need, adding them in minute quantities to the colour on your glass, and test repeatedly against the colour of the porcelain until you achieve a perfect match. If you are using pigments and need to add any new colours, or you run out of a colour and need more, remember to make a paste with some uncured resin first, and then add that to the shade you are building up. It is very tempting just to add more pigment to the mixture straight from the jar, but then you run a very real risk of creating lumps of unmixed colour.

When you have achieved your perfect match, add the catalyst to the resin together with any thinners that may be needed to make your mixture workable for either a brush or an airbrush.

7 Spraying and painting

The next stage in the repair process (if you have not already colour-matched your filler resin) is to apply to the filled or replaced area of porcelain a solid colour in the form of a base coat of your resin/paint mix. To do this, you will need either an airbrush, which runs on compressed air, or, if you do not have access to this very useful but highly specialized piece of equipment, the best-quality paintbrush you can afford.

Airbrushes

For many years porcelain restorers have been using airbrushes to spray test coats, base layers, background layers and glaze coats. Airbrushes are popular because they let you swiftly apply a thin, even layer of paint, which then will be less time-consuming to smooth down than a paint layer applied with a brush.

Despite the introduction of specialized epoxies, with more restorers perfecting their skill in using coloured fills, many people still prefer to spray, or clients specifically ask for their objects to be sprayed, because if the job is well done an invisible restoration can be achieved (it is much harder to achieve invisibility with a coloured fill). If you have never used an airbrush, however, you would be well advised to read and thoroughly digest all the information and advice in this chapter before attempting to spray a piece of restored porcelain. If correctly used and maintained, an airbrush will not only give you a good result but will also enable you to do the job quickly. Uncared for or used incorrectly, however, it can all too easily become your worst enemy.

There are two main criticisms levelled at airbrushes. The first is that they constantly become blocked or clogged up with paint; the second is that they are very expensive to buy, requiring, as they do, an air compressor as well as some form of fume extraction.

To answer the first criticism the following must be pointed out. Although there is a wide selection of airbrushes on the market, produced by a variety of manufacturers, most are compatible only with watercolours, acrylics or gouache. The ones that are suitable for use with the thicker resins needed for porcelain restoration tend to have wider heads and, therefore, produce a wide spray; for porcelain repair, however, it is essential to be able to spray fine lines. What is needed is a heavy-duty airbrush, but one that will spray at least as fine as 0.4mm, if not finer. This means that the airbrushes most suitable for your purposes are going to be used for a job for which they were not designed to cope. You are, therefore, more likely to encounter problems with clogging, but only if you fail to observe the rules of care and cleaning. Restorers have only themselves to blame if the results they obtain are less than satisfactory, as all too

Health hazards: Safety precautions and equipment

It is of paramount importance to follow health and safety procedures when spraying and painting resins. Before picking up an airbrush, consider the hazards and dangers of these methods, bearing in mind the location you will be working in.

• The most obvious danger is that of fire (*see p. 11*). The resins you will be spraying and the solvents for thinning and cleaning are all highly flammable. When you spray them, they are forced into the surrounding atmosphere where they hang as small individual particles, so make sure that there is no naked flame in the vicinity. Smoking is thus strictly forbidden, and all electrical equipment – including your compressor – should be as far away as possible from your spray area.

• There is a danger from inhaling particles suspended in the air. Some plastics are poisonous or carcinogenic, making some form of fume extraction essential. Ideally this should be a spray booth or hood and an extractor plant; if these are too expensive or you do not have the necessary space a portable fume-extraction unit is a good alternative. Failing either of these, a simple extractor fan fitted into a window as close as possible to the spray area, together with a suitable mask, is far better than no protection at all.

• Even when you are using a spray booth, you may at times need to inspect an object closely while spraying it, thus exposing yourself to the risk of inhaling some of the resin particles. In these circumstances, it may be safer to use a mask as an additional precaution. Any restorer who sprays resins in a confined, unventilated room without suitable protection will, over a period of time, become increasingly likely to suffer from illnesses and allergies associated with resins. The resins and not the spraying are the prime culprits here – you must take precautions not only when spraying but also whenever you are using resins.

• Wearing goggles is not always convenient for fine work, but they will protect your eyes from any splashes of resin or solvent. Always have an eye-wash bottle in your first-aid kit and wear resin- and solvent-resistant gloves to protect your hands.

• The compressed air for your airbrush can be very dangerous if used incorrectly, even at low pressure. As little as 4 psi (pounds per square inch) can cause damage to your eyes or ear drums. Never attempt to test the jet of air by directing the pressure at your skin – pressurized air can enter your body through cuts, even hair follicles, causing local swelling that will need to be treated surgically. It can also enter your bloodstream, taking any residues of paint or resin with it, and thus cause infections or even blood poisoning.

• Do not clean your work area by blasting it with compressed air – the resultant flying debris could injure you and others working nearby. Airborne dust could also cause respiratory problems.

• Always make sure that the hose nozzle is free from dirt and moisture, then attach your airbrush to it before switching the air supply on. Turn off the air supply before changing attachments and never use more than the required air pressure.

• Have the compressor serviced regularly and always make sure that everyone using it is properly trained in its safe operation. It is also advisable to wear ear protection if your compressor is not fitted with a silencer (*for further advice on health and safety, see pp. 9–11*).

often is sadly the case. Take the trouble, then, to seek out an airbrush that is designed for spraying thicker mediums but with a fine head, and make sure you maintain it scrupulously.

If you attend an evening class, where one or two airbrushes may have to be shared among several students, it is your obligation to treat the airbrush as carefully as you would your own. If the airbrushes used in these classes survive the working year it is due to careful maintenance by every student using them. The ideal situation is to have your own airbrush, so that it becomes your sole responsibility to keep it clean and functioning properly.

Those who say that airbrushes are too expensive do have a point, but worth is relative to the needs of the individual restorer. If you are intending to become a professional, you will certainly find one useful; it will save you time (and so soon pay for itself) and if you use it properly and skilfully it will produce work of the highest standard. You can buy airbrushes from the larger specialist art and graphic shops but it would be worth contacting a retail outlet that specializes in airbrushes alone, somewhere that sells, services and gives advice on a choice of airbrushes by different makers. Iwata® and Paasche® are the two leading brands, but Aerograph® and Badger® are also well regarded.

Types of air supply

Most airbrushes use compressed gas to push the paint through the nozzle. This compressed gas is usually air; I have seen an airbrush run on oxygen but this is an expensive alternative. It is not to be recommended in any case, because the pressurized cylinder can be dangerous, not to mention a fire hazard, if handled incorrectly. The easiest ways in which you can obtain compressed air at present are by purchasing it in canned form or by using a compressor.

Canned air

One way to obtain compressed air is to buy it in an aerosol-type can. The airline of the airbrush screws into the top of the can, so check to see whether or not you need an adaptor. Although this sounds a cheap and easy way of running your airbrush, in reality it does have its drawbacks. First, the cans, available commonly in 750ml sizes – are relatively very expensive and they do not seem to last that long – one to two hours, perhaps. They are supposed to have resealing tops, but I have found that a small amount of air escapes, which reduces the lifespan of the can still further. I would recommend cans only if you intend to do very little spraying because, effectively, you will be using one can every time you spray. In the long run it would be much cheaper to buy a compressor.

Compressors

The most usual and efficient (though initially expensive) way of generating compressed air is by means of a compressor. If you intend to spray professionally the purchase of a compressor is essential. Those made by two of the big manufacturers, Badger® and Bambi®, are very difficult to get hold of now in the UK, as Badger® do not export widely out of America and Bambi® tend to manufacture larger compressors for the European market. The main producers of smaller compressors, suitable for the restorer's needs, are Iwata®, Paasche® and Aerograph®. Within each range, models vary from the simplest to those equipped with many extra features, so it is important that you consider your basic requirements before making a decision about which to buy. First and foremost, the compressor must be able to deliver adequate pressure to the head of the airbrush. Different restorers have their own preferences as to how much pressure this should be, but it should range from at least 25 up to 40 psi. If necessary it should have the capacity for more than one airbrush to be used at the same time. Ideally it should also be lightweight, compact and (preferably) quiet. Safety features, such as an electric cut-out pressure switch, should also be considered.

Compressors can be either of the oil-less diaphragm type or oil-filled; the two work in quite different ways. Oil-less compressors produce a lower pressure, on

Useful features

Some of the smaller, cheaper compressors will not have the following very helpful features, but you may be able to get them as attachments. It is worth bearing in mind, though, that adding more than one or two of these to an oil-less diaphragm compressor will bump the price up to such a degree that it would probably be more cost effective to purchase an oil-filled one anyway.

Regulator with gauge This will tell you the pressure at which the compressor is working (and let you know if it is working at all) and also enable you to regulate the amount of air going into the airbrush. You can thus lower the pressure if you want to obtain a very fine line and increase it if you want to spray large areas of fill.

Air filter and moisture trap The air filter removes large particles of dust. This saves you ending up with a finish that feels like sandpaper and needs a lot of rubbing down. The moisture trap reduces the air humidity a little and prevents water droplets from appearing on your sprayed surface. It is possible to buy a combined gauge, air filter and water trap.

Reserve tank This refinement – a reserve tank in which the compressor stores the air – has two advantages: it gives a very steady flow of air to the airbrush and it allows more than one airbrush to be run off the same compressor. This is worth considering if you already have the above extras and intend to run a workshop that will require more than one airbrush in operation at the same time.

average 35 psi, but a higher volume of air. They do not always have reserve tanks, moisture or filtration facilities, although you could possibly have these fitted. They are maintenance free and relatively inexpensive to buy.

Oil-filled compressors are much heavier pieces of equipment and are operated on a piston and motor system, very much like a car piston. They work on a much higher pressure and lower volume of air, and so are ideal if you want to use more than one airbrush at a time. Reserve tanks, filtration and moisture filters ensure that they provide a steady flow of clean, dry air. However, being oil-filled they do need regular maintenance (about once a year) and the oil is not cheap. Although they are much more expensive to buy, they are silent to run – a feature that many people consider a priority.

Once you have your compressor and airbrush, it would be a sensible idea to practise spraying at different pressures until you feel fully in control. I was brought up with a compressor capable of producing 100 psi and became accustomed to spraying very fast at 35 to 40 psi. However, if you start by spraying at a lower pressure, you will soon get used to it and will probably dislike the fast-spraying pressure.

Types of airbrush

I have been using airbrushes for fifteen years and have tried many different makes, but my favourite is still the Conopois®. Though Conopois® airbrushes have not been made since 1988 they are still considered by ceramic restorers to be among the best. Consequently they still have an excellent second-hand market and you can get spare parts and have them serviced at specialist centres. The Badger® 100 series is still available, too, but the most popular airbrushes these days are made by the Japanese company Iwata® and the American company Paasche®. It is not only important to know how to use an airbrush but also vital to be able to recognize the correct type for your needs. So before buying, as with the compressor, you need to consider what your requirements are.

Airbrushes all have optional trigger mechanisms, which divide into two groups – double or single action. With double-action models, the trigger/button is pressed down to release the air and pulled backwards to release the paint all in one action and with one hand, allowing you to control the air pressure and the amount of paint released simultaneously, and making it easier to achieve fine lines and apply an even or varied depth of colour.

With a single-action model, these two operations are controlled by separate mechanisms: you adjust the paint flow first with one control lever and then press a button to release the air.

Cups and mixing

Another factor to consider is whether the cup is detachable or fixed. There are two main types: gravity feed or siphon feed. The air and paint in the brush can also be mixed in one of two ways: internally or externally.

Gravity feed

These have fixed cups on top of the airbrush. The paint is drawn to the head partly by gravity, so less air pressure is required and the action is correspondingly slower.

Siphon feed

These have detachable cups fitted to the side of the airbrush. They use more air, thus allowing you to work a little faster. You can also angle the airbrush for awkward areas, as the cup can be twisted in any direction. This flexibility enables you to work with a cup of thinners next to the airbrush so that if it becomes blocked you will be able to flush it through without having to remove all your paint first. In addition, if you require more than one colour you can have them ready prepared in separate cups.

Internal mix

Here, the paint is mixed with the air inside the airbrush head so that on release it is thoroughly atomized into microscopic dots of colour, producing a flat, even layer of paint.

External mix

In this design, the paint and the air are mixed together as they leave the airbrush head so that much coarser paint droplets are laid down, making it impossible to achieve a fine line. Since you will need an airbrush that can spray finely, you will almost certainly opt for an internal-mix model in any case.

Whether you choose a double- or single-action model, a gravity or siphon feed or an internal- or external-mix design is very much up to you. If you have a chance to try out the various types before making a decision, you will have a clearer idea of which model you will be most comfortable working with.

Makes of airbrush
Conopois®

The Conopois® F model (*see p. 116*) is, in my opinion, the best of the older designs ever to have appeared on the market, fulfilling as it does all the functions I need in an airbrush. As originally produced, it came in a box with spare plastic colour cups, a hand-extension tube, nozzle remover and three specialist cups – a small paint cup, a large one and a split-level cup – and, most important of all, a spare needle. My regard for the Conopois® lies in its adjustability. It is a single-action, siphon-feed airbrush: the air flow is adjusted by means of a screw at the base of the trigger; the paint flow is controlled by a ring setting just behind the trigger area. It has four levels for spraying, from fine to three. It also has a safety setting that retracts the needle into the airbrush, so preventing it from becoming damaged during storage. The airbrush is not really

RIGHT A Conopois® single-action, siphon-feed airbrush (*top*), and an Iwata® HP-C double-action, gravity-feed airbrush (*bottom*).

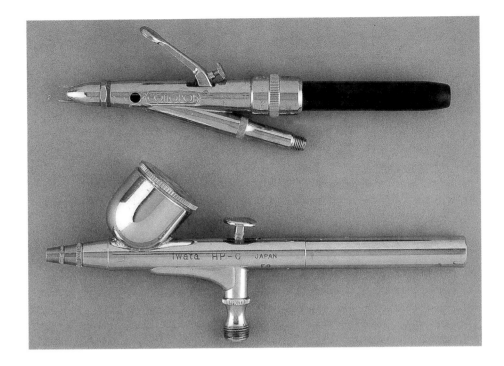

supposed to be operated on this setting, but I like to use it when I want to spray coarse and fast. It has detachable cups and an attachment called a stipple cup, which sprays a range of textures from small dots to a coarse splutter. If you are left-handed, this airbrush presents no problem: it has holes for the colour cup on either side, so you can choose the side that suits you best. The side you don't use must have the socket plug in place or the brush will not spray properly, but the feature does allow you to spray two colours at once, should you need to.

In my opinion there are two problems with the Conopois® airbrush, but only because it is routinely used for resins, for which it was not designed. Just behind the entry hole for the colour cup is a fibrous washer, and this is affected by the solvents we use. In fact, it dries up and shrinks, and eventually has to be replaced. Unfortunately, this involves returning the airbrush to the manufacturer (or, since this machine is no longer made, to a specialist service centre). If you want to avoid, or at least postpone, changing the washer, you have to oil it much more frequently than the rest of the mechanism, and sometimes this oil does interfere with the resin sprays.

The other problem is that you cannot penetrate to the middle of the airbrush to clean the trigger mechanism in the same way as you can with other makes of airbrush. If the airbrush is treated correctly, there should never be any need to do this, but just occasionally new students make mistakes, and it would be helpful to be able to examine it thoroughly. I can understand, however, the view expressed by Conopois® that if new students get inside the spring-loaded middle section they would be likely to find themselves in great difficulty.

Badger®

Badger® airbrushes are produced by a large American company but are not widely distributed in Great Britain, though you should be able to obtain them from good art or graphic shops. The 100 range has a double-action and the 200 range a single-action mechanism.

The model I am familiar with is the 100SF, which is a double-action, siphon-feed airbrush. It is a simpler airbrush than the Conopois®, in terms of both what it can do and its mechanism. It is available in right- and left-hand models, with fine or medium heads. The colour cups are all metal and have bases that you can unscrew for easy cleaning. As the centre and back sections of the airbrush are removable, they can be cleaned if necessary, whereas those on the Conopois® cannot.

Iwata® HP-B, HP-C and HP-SB

Iwata® make the finest airbrushes on the market today. Many different designs are available but the HP-B, HP-C and HP-SB are best suited to the restorer's needs. They all have a double-action mechanism, so the level of paint flow and air pressure are controlled by the same lever. The HP-B and HP-C (*see opposite*) are both gravity-feed airbrushes with the cups attached. The HP-SB, though a siphon-feed model with a removable metal cup, is in other respects very similar in design to the HP-B and the HP-C. The HP-B will perform well with slightly less pressure and can produce medium to fine lines, down to 0.2mm. The HP-C model sprays broad to fine, down to 0.3mm, but it can be fitted with an HP-B nozzle to achieve finer lines; equally the HP-SB sprays medium to fine, down to 0.2mm, but can be interchanged with the HP-C nozzle to achieve a wider spray.

Cross-section through a Conopois® airbrush

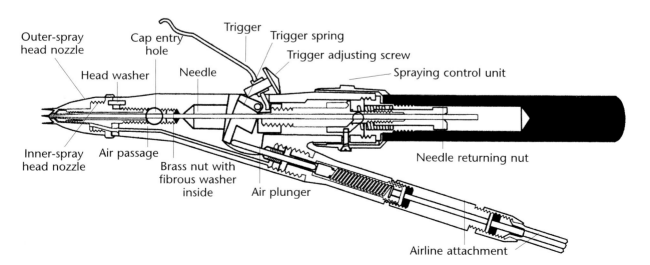

Although the HP-SB removable cup feature makes this model very flexible, like the Conopois®, enabling you to flush it with thinners and use different colours easily, the HP-B and HP-C fixed cups are very easy to keep clean and are less prone to clogging than other types of fixed-cup design. The HP-C model is the most versatile of the HP series of airbrushes because it has a bigger cup and a wider nozzle. The HP-SB, like the Conopois®, allows you to attach the cup to either the left- or the right-hand side of the airbrush. All give excellent performance. The HP-B is the least expensive of the models; the HP-SB the most expensive.

Paasche® V, VL

Paasche® produces a wide range of airbrushes; the V and VL models being the most suitable for porcelain restoration. They are both double-action, siphon-feed models with metal cups. The V model can produce only a fine to medium spray, whereas the VL is extremely versatile, producing fine lines through to a much broader spray. Different-sized colour cups can be obtained for both. The V comes in a left-handed version – VV; the VL is suitable for both left- and right-handed people. The VL is available with three different-sized heads – 1, 3 and 5 – according to the thickness of the spraying medium. Fluids of medium and heavy viscosity require sizes 3 and 5, respectively; they also need different-sized air-caps, tips and needles. The VL is considered a heavy-duty airbrush but the fine nozzle still goes down to 0.4mm. They both come boxed with appropriate accessories: metal cup, head protector cap and (with the VL) an extra needle and extra tip.

How an airbrush works

It is important to understand how an airbrush works for two reasons: if the appearance of the sprayed area is not as you want it, knowing about the paint/air relationship will help you remedy the situation; and if something goes wrong with the airbrush you will know how to track down the fault.

An airbrush may be divided into four areas of action (*see p. 117*):

1 Front nozzle or head
2 Paint-entry point
3 Trigger and air entry
4 Needle-holding area

In very general terms, the paint is sucked into the airbrush by compressed air, which is then forced out of the front nozzle drawing the paint with it.

General overview

To operate the airbrush, connect it to the air supply and fix the colour cup in place. Now press the trigger. This simple action causes a number of things to happen at once. It pushes down the spring-loaded plunger, thereby allowing air to rush along the air channel into the space between the outer and inner heads. At the same time the trigger, which is also holding the needle (each airbrush has its own mechanism for this process), pushes it back, thereby opening a hole in the outer head through which the compressed air escapes. As this air escapes, it sucks first the air then the paint in the paint-entry area along the colour-cup channel into the airbrush and along the needle to its tip, where the air-and-paint mix is forced out through the inner spray-head nozzle. When the trigger is released, the needle, which is itself spring-loaded, moves forward and closes the exit hole in the head. The plunger rises and shuts off the air, but the paint between the entry hole at the side and the head exit is trapped, and this is where most of the problems associated with airbrushes normally begin.

To this simple explanation of airbrush action, several points must be added. If the needle is positioned a fraction further back, the exit hole becomes larger, with the result that more paint will escape. If the trigger is pulled further back, there is a resultant increase in both air and paint. You can also increase the air pressure and, therefore, use more air with the same amount of paint. All these variables combine to make the airbrush a highly complex tool with very individual characteristics.

Just how you adjust your airbrush depends on the viscosity of the medium being sprayed. As porcelain restorers tend to use resins and paints that are more viscous than those intended by the manufacturers of many airbrushes, there are danger points within any airbrush. The most vulnerable are without doubt those in the two sections of the head where nearly all the 'work' of the airbrush is done. The exit hole for the paint is so small that even a grain of pigment may block it. If it is not cleaned properly, thin layers of paint build up around the inside of the head and make it completely useless. The outer head is also vulnerable – paint may well run back down the channel and harden once the air is shut off. Another difficult area is the long needle, for any paint left on it will prevent it from moving backwards and forwards properly. It is also very finely ground at the tip to match the size of the exit hole and this tip is, unfortunately, extremely accident prone, as it can very easily become bent. Once it is bent, the airbrush will never really work effectively until it is replaced. Any attempt to straighten it is likely to be a waste of effort and could cause damage to the bearing washer and the inside of the inner head.

Preparation and assembly

Before you even attach the paint cup to the airbrush there are a few steps you should take to ensure that it is working properly. The airbrush will probably have been dismantled into sections for storage, so your first task is to assemble the necessary components – the main body, airline, needle, inner and outer heads, washers and plugs, and at least two colour cups. You will also need thinners and thick paper tissues (never use cotton wool, as fibres can get into the mechanism). The airbrush should have been thoroughly cleaned after its last use, but it is worth checking before you start spraying, especially if you share it with other restorers. Each make of airbrush may require slightly different procedures, so it is very important to read the information supplied with your airbrush. The following information is general to all.

Colour cups

If you have detachable cups, unscrew the base (if it is separate) and remove any trace of paint from the inside using thinners and tissues. You may have to scrape the base with a spatula to remove all of the paint. On the Conopois® cup, you need to remove a small screw at the base of the paint channel; feed thin fuse wire down the channel to remove any paint. Replace the base, half fill the cup with thinners and then tip the cup up so that the exit tubes point downwards – there should be a fairly fast flow of thinners droplets. If so, the cup is ready for use.

Body

The design of the airbrush body varies according to make and to whether the mechanism is double or single action. All makes have a metal or plastic casing that can be removed from the back of the body to reveal the needle chuck. Test the trigger or lever by pressing down (and pulling back if it is a double-action model) and then let go – the trigger should respond with a fast, smooth return. You should also be able to see the needle move backwards and forwards smoothly as you adjust the trigger.

If any of the actions are not smooth, or the trigger stays in the open position, clean the trigger area with thinners and oil if required. Finally, make sure that the colour cup entry hole is free of paint.

Head

It is a good idea to store the head (but not the entire airbrush) in a small bottle of thinners. The head should be broken down into the inner and outer parts if it has two components. The outer head must be checked for paint on the outside and inside surfaces, particularly round the exit hole. The inside, because of its smaller size, is more difficult to deal with – in terms both of detecting any traces of paint and then of cleaning them out. If there is any paint present, place your finger over the exit hole to prevent the thinners running out (remember to wear gloves) and clean the paint away with a tissue and thinners. You can use a paintbrush for this instead of a tissue if you prefer, but whichever method you use make sure no trace of paint is left inside.

The inner head is much more difficult to inspect. First of all, examine the small hole in the collar through which air passes to the air chamber and check that it is not blocked. Take the airline and use a little compressed air to blow out any blockage. Hold the head up to the light and see if any light is visible through the end. If it is blocked you may be able to clear it using a spent spray

---

Fitting a Conopois® needle

This operation can be tricky, as the needle has to pass through a number of obstacles. You need to be extremely careful when passing the needle through the trigger area, but the biggest danger to its fine point is the fibrous washer that sits just behind the socket plug – if this washer has started to break up, then the needle is likely to become snagged in passing and be diverted into the side wall, becoming bent in the process. Once the needle is successfully in place, tighten the needle nut so that it grips the needle very firmly. Raise the trigger to its full position and then push it down – the needle nut and needle should both move backwards. If only the nut moves, tighten it a little more and try again. If the needle still fails to move, it is being held back either by paint or because the leather washer has shrunk. If paint is the culprit, remove the needle and clean it with thinners. If the fibrous washer is clinging to the needle, you have a more difficult problem. Try re-oiling the airbrush and allow it to stand for at least an hour before testing the needle again. If this fails, you will need to return the airbrush to a specialist service centre to have the washer replaced.

---

needle. Carefully push the needle into the head and check to see if it comes out of the end – just the tip should protrude. It is advisable, however, not to do this too often, as it tends to have the effect of enlarging the spray head.

Next, screw the inner and outer heads together once more and replace the head washer, if there is one. Screw the head assembly into the body and tighten it with the tool provided. Do not tighten it to such an extent that you crush the head washer – if you do, the flow will be cut off.

Needle

Unscrew the needle chuck and slowly pull out the needle. Inspect it for any paint residue or clear resin by running your fingernail down the side, avoiding the very delicate tip of the needle. If it does need cleaning – you may have to soften the paint with thinners first – wipe it with a tissue moistened with thinners. Always pull the needle through the tissue backwards to prevent any possible damage to the tip. Replace the needle in the airbrush by pushing it gently until it appears at the head, then tighten the needle chuck. Pull the trigger back and check to see that the needle is retracting smoothly into the airbrush. If not, retighten the chuck and test it again.

If, at this point, it is still not retracting you will have to remove the needle, since very probably there is still some rogue paint somewhere inside the airbrush assembly that is causing it to stick. If there is no trace on the needle, it may be the front part of the airbrush that needs cleaning. Be sure to check the manufacturer's instructions to see whether the needle should be stored in or outside the airbrush (*see box above for more details*).

Troubleshooting – Airbrush problems

Problem	Cause and remedy
The air is not coming out of the head, although it is coming out of the air valve.	• The head washer has been overtightened and the air-passage holes have been crushed shut. If so, loosen the head washer. • The air-exit hole in the inner head is blocked with paint or the air hole in the washer is not in line. If so, remove the paint or realign the washer. • The plunger in the air valve is stuck and the trigger is having no effect on it (generally this plunger tends to jam open). If so, loosen the valve screw and release plunger and spring. Take care when opening, as the plunger is spring-loaded. • Old paint has built up around the exit hole, preventing the air from escaping. Clean it with thinners or, as a last resort, paint stripper.
Thinners does not come out when the trigger is pushed down.	• Blockages can occur at the colour pot – look in the pot hole to see whether or not thinners is coming into the airbrush. If not, change the pot and place the old one in a container of thinners. The spray heads can also become blocked – if necessary, remove and clean them. • This problem can also occur if you fail to replace the plug in the unused colour pot socket or, less commonly, you fail to put the needle in.
Air bubbles up into the colour cup.	This fault is most commonly caused by overtightening the head washer, with the result that some of the air escapes through the head but some forces its way back down the needle and into the colour cup. Slacken the head washer and release the needle, then correct its setting into the head.
The thinners comes out in fits and starts in a spitting fashion.	• This is usually caused by a blocked head or when the inner and outer heads do not match (the interchanging of parts may cause all manner of problems, as the airbrush is a finely tuned piece of machinery). Clean the head; make sure the inner and outer heads are from the same airbrush. • This problem can also be caused by a sticking needle, which is normally the result of paint on the face of the socket plug. If this is the problem, remove the socket plug and clean it.
There is a loss of or decrease in air pressure.	• First, remove the airline from the compressor, then switch on the compressor and satisfy yourself that it is functioning as it should. There should be sufficient air being blown from it. If there is anything wrong with the compressor it is best to contact a professional repairer. • Next, check the airline itself for any leaks by running your hand along its length. If you find one, repair it or better still replace the airline. Leaks from connections, such as the male and female brass connection, can be remedied

Problem	Cause and remedy

There is a loss of or decrease in air pressure (*continued*).

simply by tightening. If this fails, try wrapping some plumbers' plastic tape around the thread and retighten.

• Check the air-intake filter, which often becomes blocked. If it is hard or dirty, replace it.

• If air is coming through the airline as it should, connect the airbrush and remove the outer head. Press the trigger. If air comes out, then the inside of this outer head is probably blocked with paint. If so, clean and reassemble it. If the air flow is still reduced, test again with the head removed.

• If you still have no luck, then the problem you are experiencing must lie somewhere between the airline joint and the front exit. The air valve is one of the main problem areas in an airbrush. The spring that operates the valve sometimes sticks and prevents the plunger from coming down and releasing air into the airbrush and through the head washer. Undo the valve housing and release the valve.

• Finally check the head washer; if the head is screwed on too tight, the holes in the washer through which the air passes will be crushed shut, and the air supply will be severely restricted or even completely blocked. This often, although not always, causes the air to blow back as described below. Loosen the head to relieve some of the pressure on the washer and test again. If all is not well, you will probably have to replace the washer.

There is air blowing back into the colour cup, reducing or stopping the paint flow.

• If the head of the airbrush is screwed on too tightly it could have crushed the washer. This stops all the air flowing through the washer to the spray head, and some of it finds a new route – along the needle and into the paint channel. Loosen off the head and replace the washer if necessary.

• A dirty needle has the same effect. Ease the pressure on the washer and clean the needle.

You are experiencing 'stop-start' spraying

The most common reason for this is a sticking needle caused by resin build-up in the needle channel. It could also be due to interference with the air supply at the inner head section. Cleaning these sections usually remedies the problem.

There is no paint coming into the airbrush.

It is often tempting when an airbrush refuses to spray to take it to pieces, but this can be a costly mistake. Check to see whether paint is actually entering the airbrush. Remove the colour cup and look into the hole. If the hole is not completely filled with paint the paint is not coming through the cup correctly. To remedy, clean or replace the cup.

There is air coming out of the head, but no paint.

The reason for this could be found among the faults already outlined, such as blocked paint channels, dirty heads, blocked colour cups, and so on. There is,

Problem	Cause and remedy
There is air coming out of the head, but no paint (*continued*).	however, a more common reason that affects two vital actions of the airbrush simultaneously. After cleaning a Conopois® airbrush, you may not have replaced one of the colour cup socket plugs, with the result that no paint is pulled down the needle. For the same reason the needle does not retreat and so blocks the exit hole for the paint. Replace the missing part.
There is a large amount of paint in the back of the airbrush around the trigger area, causing it to stick.	Small amounts of paint will always make their way to the back of the airbrush when paint-covered needles are withdrawn for cleaning. Large amounts of paint should not, however, be present. If they are, then the seal at the back of the colour cup is probably at fault. Unless you are a truly experienced airbrush engineer, you should return the airbrush to the shop where you bought it, or to the manufacturer, for an overhaul.
The paint sprays to one side, not directly from the centre of the head.	It is essential to be able to anticipate where the paint will come from when it leaves the airbrush. Occasionally you will find that the paint sprays to the left or right of where it should. The cause of this problem is likely to be a bent needle. If this is the case, change the needle or try to straighten it. Attempts at straightening are, however, rarely successful.
A thin spray or only a small amount of paint comes from the airbrush.	• The most common cause of this defect is a thin layer of paint building up between the inner and outer heads. As the exit hole for the air and the paint is narrowed, the amount issuing from the airbrush is reduced. • Another cause might be that the needle returning nut might not have been tightened sufficiently, with the result that when the trigger is pulled back the needle retreats only a short distance. To rectify this, replace the needle in the correct position, tighten the nut and clean the inside of the outer head and the tip of the inner head.

Testing the airbrush

Once the airbrush is assembled, refit the metal or plastic back, connect the brush to the airline and switch on the air supply. If a reserve tank is fitted, allow it to fill. Push down on the trigger (to expel any storage solvent) and the air should flow freely from the head. Examine all the connections for air leaks – airbrush to airline, and airline to compressor. The two most common points where air escapes are the airline connection and the spray-head washer. With practice you will know if the correct amount of air (depending on the pressure at which you have set your compressor) is coming out of the airbrush. Half fill a colour cup with thinners and push down fully on the trigger – the flow of thinners should be fast and furious, though not flooding. Now press the trigger

Improving your accuracy

If you are new to airbrushing there is a game you can play that will help you to improve the accuracy of your work.

• On a piece of card, draw ten small circles – about the diameter of the end of a pencil. Now spray thinners at the centre of each one. When you can hit dead centre on all ten circles, holding the airbrush about 5cm (2in) away, reduce the size of the circles and try again. Only when you can hit each tiny spot with the shortest of trigger pauses should you consider yourself really qualified to spray a piece of porcelain.

Here is a second learning game you can also try to sharpen your airbrushing skills.

• Draw a square with sides about 2.5cm (1in) long on a piece of stiff card and try to spray it with paint. Your first attempt will probably fail in two respects: a lot of spray is likely to fall outside the box area, and what paint lands inside is likely to be patchy. The first fault is due to a lack of judgement of distance. An airbrush emits the paint from its nozzle as thousands of small particles: the further you move the airbrush from the paper, the wider the spray arc; the further from the centre of the spray, the further apart these particles land. At the edges of the sprayed area, they appear as individual dots. To remedy this fault, spray round the edges of the square with the airbrush close to the paper and the pressure reduced. When you have covered the edges of the box, move the airbrush back from the paper a little, increase the pressure and spray the centre. The second fault – patchy paint distribution – is caused by passing the airbrush unevenly over the surface you are working on. This is corrected by learning the correct technique and then practising it over and over again.

• There are two ways to move the airbrush when spraying: both are in general use and both are effective. The first might be called the 'straight line' technique. To spray a square, first spray around the border; then spray a line just below and slightly overlapping your first spray line, and work your way down. When the whole area has been covered, spray between your original spray lines. This technique ensures even and total coverage.

I personally find this a rather fussy method and tend to favour the second technique, which involves using the airbrush in a circular motion. Start in a corner and, using very tiny circular movements, apply the paint evenly. It is at first sometimes a little difficult to see how you are getting on – the circular motion of the airbrush does occasionally obscure the surface you are painting. After practice, however, most students tend to favour this technique.

with more control: if you are using a double-action trigger, press and pull back; if you are using a single-action model, alter the paint release before pressing the trigger. A fine, even flow of thinners should be coming out, without spitting, 'stop-starting', or air bubbling up into the colour cup. If any of these problems occur, they must be remedied (*see pp. 122–4 for airbrush problems*).

If you clean the airbrush after spraying, and then check again during assembly prior to your next spraying, you should have few problems. If you do encounter any the information supplied with your airbrush will provide some guidance on problems and remedies. The Troubleshooting chart (*starting on p. 122*) applies to a Conopois® F model, the airbrush I am most familiar with, but you should find that much of the information applies to other makes.

Using the airbrush

Once you are happy with the way your airbrush is working, mix your resin and paint together and thin to the required consistency. The mixture should be thin enough to let the paint flow through the airbrush but not so thin that the paint loses its covering power. As a general guide, add about 25 per cent or less of thinners, never more. Half fill the colour cup with the paint mixture, but not more than half or you will find it tipping out over the edge of the cup if you angle the airbrush incorrectly. Now carry out a test spray on some newspaper. The paint should cover the black print after three or four passes of the airbrush. If it does not then the paint lacks sufficient covering power, and so many coats will be needed to cover the repair that its surface will look bumpy compared with that of the original. The paint should also be spraying evenly over the paper; if it is not, check the Troubleshooting charts (*see pp. 122–4 and 128–9*) and correct the problem accordingly.

Once everything is running smoothly, adjust the airbrush and air pressure to obtain the degree of coverage required. It is a good idea, if you are using an airbrush with detachable cups, to have a cup of thinners to hand. This cup has two functions. First, it enables you to drop small amounts of thinners into the paint colour cup to thin it, which is a very controlled way of thinning paint as the thinners cup acts like a pipette; second, if any blockage occurs while you are spraying, the thinners in this cup can be sprayed to clean out the airbrush.

Spraying technique

In comparison with the minute attention to detail that is necessary when you are preparing to spray, the actual process of spraying itself is relatively easy – provided, of course, that your airbrush is working perfectly. There are, however, certain rules that you must observe.

1 You, the sprayer, should always know exactly where the paint is going to land when it comes out of the airbrush.

2 You must keep the airbrush constantly on the move during the spraying process. If it is stationary, the paint will very quickly build up and create a 'starfish' effect or a paint run. The speed at which the airbrush should be moved is usually very slow but will be governed to some extent by the pressure of the air: the greater the air pressure, the faster the movement.

To become expert will require practice, as control of the speed at which you move the airbrush and the accuracy with which you can aim it are the two elements that make up good spraying – see 'Improving your accuracy' (*p. 125*).

When you come to paint over a repaired break, you will need to spray in a narrow line and the air pressure should, accordingly, be low – somewhere between 15 and 20 psi. Hold the airbrush close to the object, about 1–2.5cm

(⅓–1in) away. If you are using a Conopois® airbrush, the setting should be between fine and 2, depending upon the viscosity of the paint/resin mix. If, however, the area to be sprayed is a large in-fill, then the exact opposite applies: the air pressure should be high, somewhere between 35 and 45 psi, and the airbrush should be held 7–10cm (3–4in) away from the surface. On the Conopois® the setting for this sort of operation should be 3 or 'safe'.

The viscosity of the paint/resin mix is an important factor: the thicker the mix, the harder it is for it to pass through the airbrush. If you are spraying a crack with too thick a mix and the air pressure is low, the paint/resin mix will either not come out of the airbrush at all or it will do so in what we term an 'orange-peel' effect – in other words, bumpy. To overcome this problem you should add a little thinners, but not so much that the covering power is reduced. You may also need to increase the air pressure slightly to ensure a dense enough coverage. These alterations of pressure, viscosity, distance and airbrush setting should all be tested on a piece of newspaper until you have everything correctly adjusted. For general spraying, which falls between the two extreme examples cited, the pressure should be 30–35 psi, the distance 5–6cm (2–2⅛in) and, on a Conopois®, the airbrush setting should be between 2 and 'safe'.

One final but very important point to remember when spraying is that you should try to keep the airbrush the same distance from the object throughout the process. If the article has a depression, move the airbrush in; if it has a protrusion, move it out. It is most important to do this, otherwise the paint will not be evenly distributed.

Spray shields

There is one more topic that has to be covered before you start to spray – the use of a shield against overspray. As the paint is pushed out of the airbrush, it travels until it finds something to land on. If you are spraying, for example, the arm of a figure and are not using a shield, some of the body will become covered in paint, which you will then have to remove. If you are spraying the rim of a cup or bowl, some of the paint will pass over the rim and settle on the other side of the object. The use of a card shield will reduce, if not completely eliminate, this unwanted spray. You need to hold the card behind the area to be sprayed and in front of any areas needing protection. Try not to place the card directly on to the porcelain, leaving it there while you spray, as the edge of the card will tend to leave hard lines of paint at any points of contact. Hold the shield in your hand and move it around – trying to keep the centre of the card in line with the centre of the spray.

There are other types of spray shield you can use, depending on the job in hand, the most common one being masking tape. Avoid using Sellotape® as its transparency makes it easy to overlook and it can, as a result, be left on the porcelain by mistake. Apply the tape in overlapping strips, covering the areas where any overspray is likely to occur. Masking tape is a very effective shield,

Troubleshooting – Spraying problems

Fault	Cause and remedy
There is water on the surface of the paint layer.	This problem usually occurs when you are using a compressor without a moisture trap. The compressor draws in air from the room, which contains a varying amount of water vapour. This builds up as water droplets in the airline and they are eventually pushed through the airbrush along with the paint. These droplets on your painted surface can make a hole in the paint when it dries and they may also run down the surface of the paint, causing streaks. Try to remove them before the paint dries; use the corner of a tissue, taking care not to disturb the painted surface. Then spray thinners through the airbrush to clean out the watery paint, disconnect the airline and change the filter. When the spraying is complete, dry out the compressor. The best way to prevent these droplets from forming is to purchase a moisture trap.
Black or coloured dots appear on the surface of your work.	Usually, coloured dots appearing on the painted surface are caused by pigments that have not been properly mixed. Some colours unfortunately never mix properly and always cause pigment dots. *Terre verte* is probably the worst offender I know of. If the problem arises when you are using a colour that is not known for this fault, you must return the paint to the colour-matching glass and crush the pigment more thoroughly. If you are encountering a problem with a renowned offender, such as *terre verte*, try a similar colour or use an oil-based paint instead (though this may involve changing your base resin). If you are using a Conopois® airbrush, black dots on the surface may be caused by the break-up of the fibrous washer behind the colour cup. If this is the case the washer must be changed.
Even after three or four layers of paint have been applied, the repair is still visible.	The paint/resin mixture does not contain enough of the base colour in relation to the amount of resin. When the very thin base layer is sprayed it therefore does not have the strength to cover. The problem may also be caused by over-thinning of the paint/resin mix prior to spraying. If the latter is the cause the situation is usually remedied by the addition of more of the original paint mix. The airbrush mechanism should be adjusted to allow more paint to flow through, thereby reducing the need for thinners. Some thinners will, of course, always be required, but the amount can be varied. You will see that it is not a good idea to pour all the colour into the colour cup at once, but to keep some unthinned paint mix in reserve in case it is needed. If insufficient base colour in the resin is the problem the solution is much more drastic: return all the mixture to the mixing glass and add more base paint. If you have already used it all, you will have to remix the colour; and if pigments have been used to tint or shade the base colour, they will also have to be added. This can be a time-consuming and costly error.

Fault	Cause and remedy

Paint runs into heavy lines or blobs.

These problems are caused by over-application of paint or by holding the airbrush stationary while spraying.

'Starfish' rings appear.

The cause is the pressure of the air as it hits the object being sprayed. If it is excessive the paint hits the surface too hard and spatters into a chain of rings, known as 'starfish'. You have some areas with little or no paint covering them and others with an excess. You should be able to prevent this at the newspaper test stage by adjusting the air pressure. If starfish suddenly start appearing in your spraying, even though the pressure is correct, the reason is probably a lapse of concentration on your part – you may have let the airbrush wander too close to the object being sprayed and the resultant increase in pressure has forced the paint on to the surface. Once the ring has appeared, it is very easy to jerk the airbrush back and then in again in an attempt to correct the mistake. Unless you are very experienced, all this usually manages to achieve is another ring.

Always set your pressure in relation to the distance from which you want to spray before you start. If a starfish appears, there are two courses open to you. If you have enough paint left, or have only just begun to spray, remove all the paint and start again; if you don't have enough paint or have nearly finished, ignore the ring and complete your spraying. Then spray the centre of the ring to even out the coverage, allow it to dry, and smooth the ring off using polishing paper.

The sprayed surface has the appearance of orange peel.

Although attractively named, the 'orange-peel' effect is definitely a problem to avoid. The paint is too thick and so is laid down in bumps instead of a smooth, even layer. This fault can be remedied by adding a tiny amount of thinners to the paint in the cup. This will allow the bumps to merge and form a smooth surface.

There are fine dots at the edge of the spraying area, commonly called 'misting', or 'the mist line'.

As the paint or resin leaves the airbrush it fans out into a cone shape before reaching its destination. The centre of the area where the spray lands becomes evenly coated with paint or resin, but towards the outer edges the volume decreases until it is no more than a few drops of spray. These drops travel until they reach a spot just outside the main spray area. As there are not enough of them to form a mass, they remain as separate dots. The problem becomes more acute the further the airbrush is held from the object being sprayed. If you have practised the 'square' exercise (*see p. 125*) you should be able to avoid misting, or at least keep it to a minimum. Do not spray at a distance greater than you have to. Even if you have to spray a large area, start spraying at low pressure around the edges, keeping the airbrush close to the object. Then return to your usual pressure and spray the main area. If you have a fixed-pressure compressor, you will have to exert control by reducing the pressure on the trigger or setting the airbrush at fine spray. The few dots that appear can then be easily removed by rubbing down.

Fault finding by elimination

Sometimes, no matter how much cleaning and inspection you carry out, your airbrush just will not work. You have had the whole system to pieces, cleaned everything and put it back together, to no avail. You will then have to play the elimination game. Decide on the general problem area – air hose, no paint, and so on – and then try to narrow it down to the head, the air valve, the washer or the needle; if you have spares, try replacing each of these components in turn. If you are lucky you might find the offending part. If you do, inspect the part to see whether you can detect what is wrong with it, to make sure that you can spot such defects if they occur again. It is probably worth your while to have your airbrush regularly serviced by the manufacturer or the supplier.

and inexperienced restorers may find the results far more satisfactory than those achieved using a hand-held cardboard shield, even though taping is more time-consuming. Instead of using tape you can paint a (removable) rubbery substance on to the exposed areas. Artists' masking medium, rubber latex and Copydex® are all effective, but take care if you are using them on thin gold.

Closely masking off the area around a fill is appropriate for 'museum' restoration, where even the slightest overpaint is unacceptable. Even using this method you may still need to sand the edges of the sprayed area lightly.

Test coats

The airbrush is a great fault finder; because it lays down such an even layer of paint, any defects in your restoration will become all too visible. Minute holes, bumps or lines that were previously undetected by eye or touch will become apparent and will have to be dealt with before you think about mixing the correct colour. Your first sprayed layer may, therefore, be regarded as a strict test of all your repair and restoration work so far. For the first test coat, spray a thin layer of a white resin/catalyst (*see opposite, top left*). You can deal with any defects as follows.

• Very small holes, less than pin-head size, may be blasted with a heavy layer of spray paint. This fills the hole but leaves a paint ring around it. Allow the paint to harden and then rub it down with a very fine abrasive paper.
• If the hole is too large to fill with paint you will have to resort to a different technique. Allow the test coat to harden (there is no need to remove it) and then fill the defect with a fine filler. When this is hard, smooth it with a fine abrasive paper (*see opposite, top right*).
• If the hole is of greater magnitude you will have to use a hard, non-shrinking filler, but first you will have to remove the test coat of paint with a solvent before filling and smoothing down in the normal way. When you are satisfied with your efforts, allow your fill to dry and then apply another test coat.

In general, your test coat may be left as a white base colour, as it will mask uneven colours in the fill in cases where more than one type of filler has been used. The more proficient you become, the less you will have to rely on the test coat to point out the defects in your technique.

Base layers

The second layer of paint you spray will be the base layer (*see right*). A base layer is applied either as a thin layer, which serves to even out any colour differences in the filling or the repair, or as a solid base colour over which layers of thinner-coloured tints are sprayed to give depth to the finished appearance of the article. If your decoration appears to be under the glaze (not a transfer or an enamel), then you will need to paint it on to the base layer by hand

(*see p. 139*), using a paintbrush, and spray tinted glaze layers over the top to produce the effect of under-glaze decoration.

If you decided not to use a spray shield and the original porcelain has been covered by only a few spray dots, or by a very thin layer of 'flick-off' paint from the base coat you have sprayed, you can remove these, if you wish, by 'painting' them with thinners before the paint has hardened. To do this, take a reasonably fine brush, for example a size 2, a paper tissue and some thinners. Dip the brush into the thinners, wiping it on the tissue to remove any excess, then brush away the paint from the surface. Take care not to wander over the edge of your restored area, or you will create a hard line at the point of junction. Don't use too much thinners, or it may run on to the restored area and affect the paint. If you have sprayed a very thick base coat, however, removing the excess in this way will result in a ridge around the edge of the pattern. To remedy this fault, allow the paint to harden then smooth it with a very fine abrasive paper.

Tint layers

The third sprayed layer may be referred to as the tint layer. A tint layer will usually contain a colour too prominent to be mixed directly with the base colour, for it would be too strong and turn it into a completely different shade. You might use a tint layer if you had a piece of very white porcelain that had a clear glaze with a hint of blue in it. The white and not the blue would need to be the predominant colour. If you mixed the blue with the white, you would produce an opaque, pale-blue base colour. To avoid this outcome, lay the two colours down separately – spray a white base coat and then for the final layer spray a blue-tinted clear glaze very thinly over the base layer in order to give the effect of a blue-toned white.

ABOVE, TOP LEFT The restored area of the rim of the Chinese plate, sprayed with a test coat (*see pp. 71–4*).

ABOVE, TOP RIGHT Faults revealed by the test coat have been remedied with fine-surface filler.

ABOVE A base layer matching the background colour of the plate has now been sprayed on top of the test coat.

Background colour

Background colour is sprayed on prior to brush-painting an overglaze pattern or applying enamels. Background colours are usually solid colours that do not require any tints. They are not, however, always easily mixed, as you are often tricked into adding colours that are not in the background but are reflections from the colours in the pattern that you hope to duplicate.

Cleaning

The major criticism levelled at airbrushes by people who do not use them – or by people who misuse them – is that they clog up or do not spray smoothly, leaving blotches and pits. I admit that this is exactly what an airbrush will do if not properly treated or handled.

Nearly all the faults associated with airbrushes are, quite simply, due to poor cleaning or not cleaning soon enough during and after use. Many people perhaps do not realize that with some modern catalyzed resins, the resin begins to harden as soon as the catalyst has been added. If you leave the airbrush full of resin/paint while you go off for a cup of tea, answer the phone or alter the colour, the inner lining of the airbrush becomes coated with a thin layer of resin/paint, which will not be removed by thinners. Eventually, if not sooner, this will block the airbrush and necessitate a major overhaul.

There are four different levels of cleaning:
• The very temporary cleaning done after a break in spraying that has lasted only a short time (say, ten to fifteen minutes).
• The between-sprays cleaning during the working day when you know that the airbrush is going to be used again that day.
• The 'goodnight' clean, which ensures that the airbrush will be ready for the next day.
• The 'holiday' clean, when you know that the airbrush will not be used for a week or longer.

Cleaning materials and methods

All the major resin-making companies produce resin thinners or brush cleaners. In many cases, thinners are exactly formulated to enable them to mix with the constituents of the resin they accompany. I would therefore strongly recommend that you use the thinners made for the resin you are applying; use others only in an emergency (if you run out of the correct thinners, for example). Using the right thinners can make the difference between an airbrush behaving well for long periods or being a rogue from the very beginning.

Temporary cleaning
The first and simplest method of cleaning – that used for short periods between sprays – is really a matter of plain common sense. Remove the colour cup containing the paint from the airbrush and replace it with a cup of solvent. Push

down the trigger and spray until clean solvent comes out from the head. Release the trigger and remove the cup. If you do not have a detachable cup, cleaning is slightly more awkward, as you will need to empty your colour out and add thinners to the cup before spraying as above. The airbrush will then be full of solvent, which will prevent any paint/resin residue from hardening inside the airbrush. You should bear in mind, however, that thinners evaporates quite readily, so this is not a process that will prevent the paint/resin from hardening if it is left inside your airbrush for long periods.

Between-sprays cleaning

The second cleaning method applies, like the first, to all airbrushes. Where it is necessary to leave an airbrush out for a few hours (but never overnight), remove the colour cup and pour out the paint/resin mix. If you have a fixed cup, remove the paint and half fill the cup with thinners. Clean the inside of the cup with an old paintbrush and pour the dirty thinners away. Quarter fill the cup with thinners and spray until all the thinners comes out clean. This process will remove most of the paint from the spray channels of the cup and clean most of the paint from the airbrush. You can use acetone to clean the cup as a cheaper alternative to thinners, but never spray it as it will, in time, cause damage to certain parts of the airbrush. Return the colour cup to its storage jar (see 'Goodnight cleaning', below), then remove the needle and clean it. Remove the two parts of the spray head and clean the paint-exit areas before placing them into thinners. Clean the area around the entry of the colour cup. Replace the needle (if it is stored in the body) but do not return it completely; the needle should pass the trigger area but not protrude out of the headless body. Place the airbrush in a safe place where it cannot be knocked over.

Goodnight cleaning

This third level of cleaning should be followed when you are preparing the airbrush for being put away for the night or, say, over the weekend. The process does vary somewhat depending on the type of airbrush you are using – some needles are best stored inside the body, others outside, for example, so it is important to read the manufacturer's literature concerning cleaning and storage that was supplied with your particular airbrush. The following, however, applies generally to all makes of airbrushes.

When you have finished spraying, remove the colour cup and clean it as before. Unscrew the bottom, if it has one, or the small brass screw (if you are using a Conopois®) and clean the channel with some thin fuse wire – this needs to be done from both ends of the channel. Refit the bottom or the screw and quarter fill the cup with thinners. Tip the cup at an angle and drops of thinners should appear at the end of the exit channel; if not, reclean. (If the airbrush is a fixed-cup design, empty the paint and flush through with thinners until it runs clear.) When it is clean, fit the cup to the airbrush and spray out the thinners.

Remove from the airbrush and clean any paint/resin from the entry point. Place the cup in a container full of thinners, along with any other used, cleaned cups – the container must have an airtight lid to prevent the thinners from evaporating. Only Teflon® plastic should be used, since other plastics may be dissolved by thinners. Glass containers are probably better in principle, but ensuring an airtight seal may then be more difficult.

Check the instructions to see how the trigger mechanism works in relation to the needle; in some designs the trigger needs to be held down while you remove the needle by unscrewing the needle chuck. Clean the needle with thinners and run your fingernail along it to see if any sticky resin is still present. Always clean from the back to the front of the needle, taking care not to damage its delicate point. Place the needle in a safe place. On the Conopois®, remove the colour cup socket plug, clean it with thinners and place it with the needle. I am always losing this plug because it is so small (and, in my airbrush, black, though red or white ones are available). You must take extra care not to do this, for your airbrush will not function without it. Now remove the spray heads and gently put the airbrush down. Unscrew the heads with the spanner provided; never use pliers. With clean thinners or acetone remove any trace of paint inside and out. A small paintbrush will help you clean the inside of the heads, but you must then ensure that you do not leave any hairs from the brush behind.

Once you have cleaned the heads, put them into thinners in their own bottle with as airtight a seal as possible. Never interchange the heads of Conopois® airbrushes; it is most important that you keep the inner and outer heads matched to the factory pairing, for if they are switched the performance of the airbrush will be seriously impaired. This is more true of the Conopois® than any of the other airbrushes.

Take a tissue and twist the corner into a point. Dip it into thinners and clean out the colour cup entry hole and the screw hole of the spray head. When all the paint is removed, replace the needle if it is to be stored in the airbrush. Stop the needle short of the front of the airbrush, which is, of course, now headless. Tighten the needle chuck. Press down and back on the trigger, thereby releasing a little air, and look at the exit hole in the front of the airbrush. If any paint is present, more cleaning will be required. If all is clean, remove the airline and place the airbrush in its box for safekeeping.

Holiday cleaning
If the airbrush is not going to be used for a week or more, follow the procedure outlined above and then take it these stages further.

How thorough your cleaning can be will, of course, depend on the extent to which you are able to dismantle the body of your airbrush. If possible, remove and clean the needle shank and spring. On some airbrushes – for example, the Badger® – you will have to fix the trigger with tape and keep the head pointed towards the floor while you release the needle chuck. You will now be able to unscrew the complete needle-spring housing. Make sure you have referred to the notes for your airbrush: with some makes, when the housing is removed you should under no circumstances place the airbrush in any position but the downward-pointing one, or the back lever will fall out and be very awkward to replace. You can clean the needle housing and spring in solvent to remove any paint from the needle channel. Once it is clean, you can oil the spring and housing (but only a small amount of oil is needed). Now screw the housing back into the airbrush, tighten the needle chuck and remove the tape.

Next, test the movement of the needle. Again, check the specification to see which parts of the airbrush should be oiled. In the Conopois®, it is necessary to oil all the working parts. The oil helps to lubricate them and also lessens the drying effect of the solvents on the fibrous washer. It is advisable to oil the airbrush at least once a month at three points: the needle nut, the trigger and the colour cup hole. The manufacturers recommend sewing-machine oil but any fine engine oil will do. Stand the airbrush in some form of container with the front nozzle pointing downwards. The oil will then flow down on to the washer and the working parts. I also oil the air-valve area. When the airbrush has stood in this fashion for about half an hour, remove it and wipe away any excess oil from the outside. Return the body to its box. I oil the airbrush without the spray head or needle in place.

Remedial cleaning

If an airbrush has become blocked with hardened paint you must resort to a more drastic method of cleaning – so drastic, in fact, that the manufacturers advise against it. The process involves the use of heavy paint strippers, such as Nitromors® or Polystrippa®, even though they can damage the washers and the plating of the airbrush. If you do decide to use a heavy-duty stripper (I tend to do so only on my training airbrush, which, owing to the inexperience of the users, sometimes demands this attention), choose Nitromors®, as it leaves less of a whitish residue.

Unscrew the head and place both halves in a small glass jar, having first removed the washer. Then cover the head with Nitromors® and allow it to stand for ten minutes. Using gloves and tweezers, remove the two parts and clean them with a paintbrush until all the paint is removed. Wipe away the paint and the stripper with a paper tissue, and then apply some more stripper. Do this until all the paint has disappeared, then clean the heads in a solvent to remove any traces of the stripper. I then oil the clean heads by gently wiping them with an oiled tissue.

The body of the airbrush may be cleaned with stripper but only from the colour cup forwards. Never allow the stripper to come into contact with the washer behind the entry hole. Apply the stripper with a paintbrush only over the relevant area. The whitish residue left by the stripper must be completely removed at the end of this process.

Paintbrushes

If you do not want to spend a lot of money on an airbrush, then you have to resort to the trusty paintbrush. Even if you do have an airbrush, you will still need to use paintbrushes sometimes – to paint patterns, for example.

Types of brush

When buying paintbrushes, you get what you pay for. There are many different types available and they differ greatly in both quality and price. The best-quality brushes are made from sable hair (kolinsky sable being the very best) and if you can afford them you will find them far superior to work with than brushes made with other hair, such as squirrel. You can get good-quality nylon brushes but they do not hold the paint as well as sable does. For painting patterns, sable is essential because the fine point on the brush not only enables you to execute very thin lines but also holds the paint in the brush-head, thus making it easier to control the flow rate. A good sable brush is also far less likely to lose its hairs than a cheaper type. There is nothing more maddening after you have spent hours painting a complicated design, with your eyes hurting and your nerves jangling as a result, than suddenly to discover a brush hair nestling within your pattern. You must then chase this rogue hair around the pattern in an attempt to fish it out, and your beautifully executed paintwork becomes a smudged, offensive eyesore. I would, therefore, advise you to buy the best brushes available. All the main art-material manufacturers supply a good range of top-quality sable brushes, capable of producing very fine lines. If properly cared for, they will last you a very long time.

Sizes of brush

Brushes range in size from 000 to 12 – the higher the number, the larger the brush. They also come in different series depending on the quality and shape; Winsor & Newton® series 7 brushes, despite having shorter hair than those in series 16, are the most expensive of all because they are made of top-quality finest sable; series 16 brushes are made from red sable, which is a little lower in quality (though still very good). If you use an airbrush to apply your base colours and require paintbrushes only to paint patterns, I would recommend that you buy numbers 0, 2, 3 and 5. Size 0 brushes are for painting very fine lines – for example, the lines on a face or the outline of a flower. Size 3 might be termed a general brush, and is used to paint lines 2–3mm (about ⅛in) thick. (If you use the tip of the brush you should, in fact, be able to paint very thin lines with any paintbrush, regardless of its size). Size 3 is also the brush most suited to painting the areas between the fine lines you have painted with your 0 brush. A size 5 brush is used to lay down larger areas of colour – for example, the coat of a medium-sized figure. If you intend to paint large areas of base colour by brush, you will require a number 7 or 8.

Techniques

When applying a base coat, it is worth while remembering one or two rules. Your brush strokes must be even – each stroke should just overlap with its neighbour. The paint should be applied lightly so as to avoid brush marks. It should never be too thick, or you will not be able to achieve an even layer. If you want an invisible restoration and are painting over the junction between the original porcelain and your repair, start by brushing along the join only, before going on to the restored area. Allow the remaining paint to stand for ten minutes or so, then add a small amount of thinners – about 10 to 15 per cent in relation to the unused paint should suffice. Then, using small brush strokes, 'feather' away the joining line between the paint and the porcelain, trying not to cover too much of the original. Allow the layer of paint to dry and then rub it down with Micro-mesh® polishing cloth until you have a surface that is completely smooth to the touch. Apply as many layers of base as you require, sanding after each one, until you have matched the original and disguised the repair. This may be anything from three to six layers. Glaze coats should be applied in the same way, but will probably require only two or three layers.

When painting with brushes it is essential to use a spatula to mix your colours into your resin, especially when using pigments that will need to be ground thoroughly. However tempting it is to add the colour medium to the resin and mix it in with the brush, this is a sure way to shorten the life of your paintbrush. The hairs will become distorted, possibly break and you will destroy the shape and fine point.

Cleaning

You will need to take good care of your brushes if you want them to last, so careful cleaning is of crucial importance. While painting, always rinse the brush in thinners between colours, using a gentle swishing movement. Resin left on a brush for even a short period of time will begin to set very quickly. Once the brush has begun to go hard, it is very difficult to restore it to its original condition. If the thinners is not effective you may have to resort to paint stripper, which, in itself, can damage the brush by loosening the hairs.

Never leave brushes standing in a pot of thinners; this treatment will cause the end of your very expensive brush to curl up. Always clean your brushes immediately after use with the correct thinners, making sure that even the thick end is clear of paint. It is also a good idea to wash them in the palm of your hand with a little washing-up liquid, gently rinsing them thoroughly with clean water afterwards. I would also suggest that you buy paintbrush hair protectors, which are clear plastic tubes that fit over the end of your brush. Paintbrushes should either be stored flat or kept upright in a container with the brush end pointing upwards.

Old paintbrushes that are past their best can always be used for jobs other than painting, such as applying consolidants, latex or paint stripper.

8 The finishing touches

Once you have prepared your object with a base coat you are ready for the final stage – painting the decoration. You should already know from earlier examination (*see pp. 25–9*) at what point in the manufacture the original decoration was applied (for example, whether it was painted under or over the glaze). If the object has not been decorated by hand, does it have a transfer? Is it enamelled or gilded? To achieve the most satisfactory results, you should apply your decoration at the same stage and in the same manner as on the original, or at least create the illusion that you have done so.

Pattern painting

Pattern painting is the process the majority of beginners fear most, and are thus reluctant to try. Their normal excuses are that they 'were never good at art' and 'cannot draw to save their lives'. When you are restoring, however, you do not necessarily have to be an artist; more often than not, you merely need to copy the design already there on the object. In many cases, painting a pattern involves no more than joining one or two lines to complete the repair. Rarely will you have to interpret the pattern completely. On occasions when you do – if, for example, a face or even an entire figure or scene is missing – you may need to do quite a lot of research in books and/or museum collections to find something suitable to copy. Only if you draw a complete blank, however, will you be obliged to rely on your own imagination. A restorer of porcelain is thus more a copyist than a creative artist. On the very few occasions when no other part of the object provides a clue and your research proves fruitless, it would be prudent to consult the owner as to what he or she would like you to do; one might give you a completely free hand while another might have definite ideas for the design, or might prefer you to leave the area undecorated.

Underglaze pattern painting

Even if you masked off the original porcelain before spraying or removed your 'flick off' paint while it was still wet, there could still be a slight ridge around the edge of the fill if you applied several layers of paint. This will need to be gently sanded flat before you paint the pattern. If you decide to leave the overspray as it is and repaint the pattern over the whole area, both original and restoration, the sprayed surface will still require very gentle sanding before you apply the decoration. A particularly busy pattern will of course help to distract the eye from the hard edge, if there is one, between the original and the repair.

If a large section of a repetitive pattern is missing – for example, around the edge of a willow-pattern plate – beware of attempting to paint it on by eye alone.

There is nothing more annoying than finding, when you are partway through your beautifully painted pattern, that there is not going to be enough space to complete it. In these circumstances, it is always tempting to 'cramp' the last part to fit the remaining space, but the results are never satisfactory. You would be better advised to 'map' the outline of the pattern on to the restored area first.

The most reliable way of doing this is to adopt your old school-day's map-making trick. Trace the pattern from a sound area of the porcelain on to tracing paper (*see above left*), turn the paper over and retrace the pattern on the other side using a soft lead pencil. Don't forget to turn the paper right side up again once you have retraced over the back, or you will end up with a reverse pattern. Then lay the tracing over the area to be repainted and trace over it again (*see above right*). Don't use a hard lead pencil with a very sharp point, as it might damage the base paint. If you use this technique, remember to blow away any excess lead particles from the surface once the pattern is drawn (*see below*). It is a good idea to keep the drawing in your file, because you might be able to use it again at some time in the future.

ABOVE LEFT A tracing of the border pattern being taken from an undamaged area of the rim of the plate.

ABOVE RIGHT The tracing in place over the restored area and the pattern being transferred.

Procedure for pattern painting

You are now ready to begin painting. Examine the original pattern, noting as many of the individual colours as possible; compare them with the colours you have at your disposal and try to decide which ones you will need and how much mixing you will have to do. If the decoration is underglaze – as it is on most porcelain pieces – its colour may be subtly, or even considerably, affected by the tint of the glaze layer (*see Chapter 6*).

BELOW With the outline of the pattern successfully transferred to the restored area, the rim of the plate is now ready for painting.

1 First, you need to make yourself a 'palette' of colours using the technique described for matching the base colour (*see pp. 106–9*). Lay out your colour medium

ABOVE The pattern has been painted on the repaired rim of the plate, which is now ready for its final glaze layer.

on the top half of the glass and your resin at the bottom. It is a good idea to use a clear resin rather than a white one and then add white colouring medium if needed. Painting patterns, especially intricate ones, normally takes much longer than spraying base colours and because the paint is being used in such small amounts it tends to dry while you are working, unless you add some thinners from time to time. You must be careful not to add too much, however, or your paint will become too thin and lose its covering power.

2 There may be several colours in the decoration; do not attempt to mix them all at once but concentrate on them one at a time. With experience, you will be able to keep the paint to a thin enough consistency while retaining sufficient covering power, although it will need a little smoothing with a very fine polishing paper or cloth. Always let your paint harden completely before smoothing, otherwise you run the risk of destroying the pattern that has taken you many hours to create (*see above*). The smoothing technique can be a very effective way of 'shading' your colours. If, for example, you have a flower that requires two or three shades of blue, removing varying amounts of paint can allow the lighter background to show through to a greater or lesser degree.

3 You will have to paint individual scenes, featuring such things as figures and landscapes, freehand, unless the piece is one of a set with the same design. One of the trickiest patterns to repaint freehand is one made up of concentric bands. This task can be made easier if you use a banding wheel. Place your object on the wheel, taking great care to ensure that it is exactly in the centre (otherwise your lines will not join up). The process is sometimes complicated by the fact that the area around which the line is being drawn is not truly circular.

4 Load the paintbrush with your mixed colour. Spin the wheel and align the tip of the brush with the end of the existing line you wish to continue. Steady your arm against your body and lower the brush so that it touches the object as it is spinning; you do not need to apply much pressure. The result should look very professional. If you do not feel confident about your ability to hold the brush steady, you can secure it in a laboratory stand and clamp. Adjust the height of the paintbrush and move the stand towards the object until the brush tip exerts exactly the degree of pressure required to give you the width of line you want. Mark the handle of the brush so that you can relocate it accurately in the clamp. Then remove it and load it with paint, reposition it in the clamp and

slowly turn the wheel until the line is complete. It may be useful to practise painting concentric lines on an ordinary white plate or saucer first, lifting and lowering the brush until you can locate the tip with pinpoint accuracy. If you do not have a wheel you will have to paint freehand but it will be much harder to achieve a professional result. Smooth the decoration flat once it is dry.

5 Another difficult effect to achieve is that often found on oriental blue and white porcelain where the blue decoration has dispersed into the glaze, creating a blurred edge to the pattern. To imitate this you can apply the overglaze before the blue has dried and delicately blend the edges of the decoration into the resin glaze with a paintbrush to create the desired effect. Alternatively, you can achieve a very good effect by using the coloured fill technique (*see p. 76*).

False glazing

When the underglaze pattern has been painted and smoothed you can apply the final layer – the glaze. The original glaze of the object you are restoring may have many individual characteristics, which you will need to note and then attempt to reproduce. It may have hardly any colour to it, in which case (unless the glaze itself is very thick) you may get away with spraying a clear resin to simulate the shine. If, however, the glaze has a definite hue (*see below*) you will probably have to tint your spraying resin to match the colour of the original. Some glazes have coloured blemishes in them, which can range in size from small dots to large patches, and to reproduce these it may be necessary to paint them on between layers of glaze.

Let us assume that the original glaze is completely clear and free from blemishes and that it has the usual high shine. Mix your false glaze and add the catalyst, apply it over the repair either with a paintbrush or by spraying (remembering to add about 10 per cent thinners) and allow this layer to set for at least twenty-four hours. Smooth down with fine polishing paper or cloth, such as Micro-mesh®, then apply a second coat leaving out the thinners (or adding as little as possible). Owing to the absence of thinners, the gloss or shine on this layer will be very high; the glaze may also, on account of its thickness, have a slightly rough surface. If so, when it is dry, rub it down until it is completely smooth. Then apply a polishing cream on a tissue (*see p. 143*); these creams are a little abrasive but polish the resin/glaze to a high gloss. Allow it to dry and then buff it with a clean tissue until you have

BELOW A tinted glaze has now been sprayed over the pattern. All that remains is to apply the decorative gilding (*see p. 145*).

the required shine. If, for some reason, your second layer is not up to standard, then you may have to spray on a third layer of resin before polishing.

Glazes that are not shiny but have a matt finish present more of a problem to the restorer. If you add a matting agent – Gasil® 23c, for example – to your ordinary glazing resin, its consistency may well become too thick for spraying. If so, you will have to apply the glazing resin with a brush. Unless this is done well, however, results are likely to be less than perfect. There are matt resins available but it is always very difficult to produce a really matt finish with them. The best choice is probably to use acrylic colours, which dry matt anyway and give a very effective matt finish when sprayed. Use the colour in the normal way, adding water as the thinner.

Crazing

Crazing, a network of fine cracks in the glaze, is caused when the glaze and the body shrink at different rates during firing. This can be a difficult effect to imitate, though the 'crackle glaze' found on Chinese ceramics, which is produced by deliberately using a glaze that does not shrink at the same rate as the body, sometimes has an oxide rubbed in to enhance the effect, creating a network of black or red lines that is somewhat easier to interpret. You can either draw the fine lines on to the false glaze with a medium-hard pencil or lightly scratch them into the surface and rub in a little of the right shade of colouring medium; a third option is to paint the lines on. To do this you will need an extremely thin solution of resin and thinners; often the dirty thinners you have been cleaning your brushes in will turn out to be just the right colour and consistency.

Using a fine brush, paint a line; then clean the brush thoroughly and with it stroke each edge of the line to remove some paint, thus making it even finer. Continue in this fashion all over the surface and the result should look very convincing. The process is, of course, extremely time-consuming. Whichever method you choose, you will need to spray a final thin glaze coat to protect your imitation crazing.

Overglaze painting

Where the decoration has been applied on top of the fired glaze (transfer or enamel), the procedures described above should be performed in the reverse order. In other words, you should apply your glaze layer first (but do not use polishing cream on the surface because it will inhibit the adhesion of the paint you use for your pattern). Once it is completely dry, you can add your decoration. A transfer-printed design will need to be smoothed down once painted; an on-glaze enamel pattern, however, will be raised above the surface of the glaze and can be quite prominent – mix your colours thickly to achieve this effect, or you could use a specialized epoxy, mixed to the correct colour and consistency using a bulking agent, so that it sits proud of the surface. Give the surface a polish once all the colours are completely dry.

Polishing creams

Solvol Autosol®

This multipurpose metal polish comes in a tube in the form of a white paste. It is quite abrasive and when rubbed between the fingers feels fairly coarse.

Pre-Lim® Surface Cleaner

This buff-coloured cream, designed for polishing cars, is supplied in screw-top metal containers of 230ml. It is only mildly abrasive and of a much smoother consistency than Solvol Autosol®.

Greygate® Plastic Polish

Greygate® has been developed specifically for use on plastics. It comes in 100ml bottles in the form of a white, very smooth, semi-viscous liquid, which needs to be shaken vigorously before use.

Renaissance® Wax

This is a microcrystalline wax polish supplied in 220ml screw-top tins. It does not contain any abrasive material, and so is more suitable for the final polish than the others described above.

You use all four polishing creams in the same way, by applying a small amount to the false glaze with a tissue and rubbing it in well. Once the surface is dry, polish with a clean tissue until you have achieved the desired degree of shine, making sure that you remove all traces of residue. If you prefer, you can use Micro-mesh® cloth for polishing, working your way through your chosen grades and finishing up with the very fine ones.

Gilding

On many repairs, the final finishing touch takes the form of gold decoration. Since such decoration was originally applied over the glaze, the modern restorer must replace it in the same way. Unfortunately, however, we cannot use the original technique, which involved firing the gold to fix it. This is because heating an object that has been restored could alter or even destroy the restoration. Original enamelling, because it is low-fired, could also be affected by heat. All the major art manufacturers produce several forms of gilding medium: gold leaf, gold transfer, gold powder, gold block, liquid leaf and gold or bronze paints and powders.

BELOW Tools and equipment used for gilding include a knife, various brushes, a gilder's cushion and books of gold leaf.

ABOVE A modern version of the 'gold repair'. The missing portion of the rim of this Chinese plate has been restored and coated with urushi (a naturally occurring resin that has been used in Japan for centuries).

ABOVE RIGHT The completed repair: gold leaf has been applied and then burnished until completely smooth. (Private collection)

Gold leaf

Gold leaf in various colours can be bought from good art shops. It comes interleaved between sheets of tissue paper in books of five sheets or more. Gold leafing is an art and, sad to say for those like myself who have not mastered it, there is no real substitute for pure gold. In my opinion, it is an art even to remove the gold leaf from its sheet without breaking it or finding that it has suddenly become airborne. Transferring the leaf to where you want it is a real skill and you can congratulate yourself if you manage to do this. The procedure may sound straightforward: coat the area to be gilded with gold size and leave it to dry for a short while so that it remains slightly tacky. Carefully cut a piece of gold leaf with a scalpel and transfer it on the end of a clean paintbrush to your piece of porcelain; static electricity will keep it clinging to the hairs. Lay it on the prepared area and brush over the surface to ensure good contact. It will stick only where the size is and you can easily brush away any excess. You can then burnish it with a burnishing stone – traditionally agate, but you can use any rounded object of suitable hardness and smoothness.

Do not be misled by this short description of gold leafing into trying it without proper instruction. To become adept in the technique you must go to a class; handling gold leaf cannot be learned from a book. Gold is very expensive, and if you have difficulty in handling it competently, porcelain restoration can become something of a financial risk. Learn how to restore porcelain, and when you have mastered this art, go to a gilding class and learn how to use gold. Meanwhile use the substitutes.

Gold transfer

Gold leaf can now be bought as a transfer, and this is much easier to apply. Coat the area to be gilded thinly with size, leave it to dry a little and lay the gold transfer over the top. Rub the back of the transfer paper with a brush or your fingers; the gold will be transferred only to the areas where the size has been painted (*see opposite*). Gold transfer will never give as good a result as pure gold leaf, however.

Gold powder or block

The next best thing to gold leaf is gold powder or block, the reason being that these are made out of real gold leaf, although it has been ground down very finely and the block has a fixative added. The solvent is usually water, and the gold can therefore be painted on to the porcelain. It dries in twenty-four hours and can then be polished. This method is expensive and the range of shades in the block is very limited.

There are two points to remember when working with gold powder or block: first, don't use too much water, or your gilding may end up with a grainy appearance; second, keep a brush solely for gilding because it will contain a quantity of minute gold flakes that may contaminate other paints or resins.

ABOVE The finishing touch: gold leaf transfer applied to the rim and the pattern.

Liquid Leaf or Treasure Gold

An acceptable method is to use gold substitutes, such as Treasure Gold or Liquid Leaf. These come in small bottles in a variety of shades and can be bought in most good art shops. On the whole, they are not a bad compromise, particularly when you consider how inexpensive they are in comparison with real gold. Before using them, make sure you mix the gold substance at the bottom of the pot very thoroughly with the fixing medium at the top. Then paint the mixture on to the porcelain with a brush in the usual way. These substances are ideal for coping with elaborate patterns. They are reasonably free from the 'graining' produced by a number of gold paints and are, therefore, ideal for beginners.

Bronzing powders

A cheaper alternative is to make up your own gold paints by buying bronzing powder, available from most art shops in a variety of shades, and mixing it with one of the resins used for false glazing. The main drawbacks you will find to this method are that the resin/gold mixture hardens to a matt finish and that, as the powder seldom mixes completely with the resin, the surface usually has a very grainy appearance. You could possibly eliminate the grainy surface by grinding the powder into your resin. Colouring agents can also be added to achieve a slightly different shade. Its only advantage lies in its cost and the ease with which the bronzing powders can be obtained.

Gold pens

Gold pens, which are widely available in art shops and general stationers, can also be used as a last resort; there is usually only one shade of gold produced by each manufacturer but you may be lucky enough to find one that matches the gilding on your piece. You will need to extract some of the gold liquid from the pen and apply it with a brush to achieve the best effect.

Conclusion

If you follow the stages outlined in this book, you should end up with a beautifully restored piece of porcelain, like the plate below. It is likely, however, that you will suffer a great many heartaches and experience horrible failures before you achieve the 'perfect finished article'. If you are very good, it will probably take three years before you can call yourself a porcelain restorer, and then only if you have proper instruction. After that, you will almost certainly have to work hard to maintain your standard. Porcelain restoration is a practical art. Although the basics can be learned from a book, if you want to know how to do the job properly, I suggest that you apprentice yourself to a professional restorer.

I still remember the awe I felt as I watched my old teacher at work: I used to marvel at the skill with which he was able to transform dirty old fragments into a beautiful piece of porcelain, bringing the object back to life. I remember how keen I was to try my hand, and recall all too well how I was duly humbled. I hope that this book will set you on the road to becoming an expert porcelain restorer. One thing is certain – if you succeed, you will find great enjoyment and immense satisfaction.

RIGHT The eighteenth-century Chinese porcelain plate fully restored. The plate is decorated in underglaze blue with a central design featuring a lotus pond with flowers, and has a dense, scrolling border. The red/orange and gilded decoration was added at a later date, probably in the West. (Private collection)

Training

Practical training in ceramic restoration can be obtained in a variety of ways; unfortunately some are very expensive. First of all you must decide what sort of training will best suit your needs. Do you intend to make a career in conservation/restoration, or are you perhaps a dealer wishing to make simple repairs to pieces to improve their appearance and saleability? Many people take up this work after retirement or as an interesting hobby for long winter evenings. Collectors who find it too expensive to have pieces professionally repaired, and prefer to spend their money on enlarging their collection, often seek help and training.

Adult evening classes run by local authorities are ideal and reasonably priced, although the amount of equipment may vary from area to area. If possible, before enrolling sit in on a class and take note of the materials and equipment used, paying particular attention to the spraying facilities. More formal courses exist, extending perhaps over a few weeks, which teach the basic techniques of repair. Like evening classes, they are a good place to meet and talk to other restorers. No course of this type, however, provides the formal qualification essential for a career in ceramic restoration. If this is what you want, you must select a full-time training course. There are no institutions that train exclusively in porcelain restoration but West Dean College, Chichester, offers a two-year course leading to a diploma in Conservation of Ceramics and Related Materials. Two-year part-time courses (accredited through the Open College Network) at Burton Manor College, South Wirral, and Urchfont Manor, Devizes, offer five or six weekends' tuition a year plus (at Urchfont) two one-week summer schools or (at Burton Manor) a first-year summer school and a second-year assessment. In addition, work in your own time is expected. Send for a prospectus for these courses to find out what they entail and their cost. Some institutions, such as museums, offer internships, although these may be available only to those who are participating in or have completed a full-time course.

Some professional restorers offer short training courses in their workshops. These may, however, prove to be very expensive in the long run, so before parting with any money be sure to obtain in writing an account of what exactly you will be taught and when. If a course lasting several weeks claims to be complete in itself, you need to establish that you will at least be taught the basic skills. Some workshops offer a series of courses, each covering a different topic in depth. In these cases you must make sure of signing up at the right time, otherwise you might have to wait quite a while before the initial course comes around again. There is little point in enrolling for a colour-matching course if you have never tackled dismantling and joining.

Useful addresses

Diploma in the Conservation of Ceramics and Related Materials
West Dean College
West Dean, Chichester, West Sussex PO18 0QZ, UK
Tel: 01243 811301
E-mail: enquiries@westdean.org.uk
Website: www.westdean.org.uk

Accredited Ceramic Restoration and Conservation Courses
Burton Manor College, Burton, South Wirral,
Cheshire CH64 5SJ, UK
Tutor: Helen Potter
Tel: 01513 365172
Website: www.burtonmanor.org

Urchfont Manor, Urchfont, Devizes, Wiltshire SN10 4RG, UK
Contact the Director
Tel: 01380 840495; Fax: 01380 840005;
E-mail: urchfont@wccyouth.org.uk

Short courses
Lesley Acton Associates, Unit 10, Bow Industrial Park, Carpenters Road, London E15 2DZ, UK
Tel: 020 8936 1111; Fax: 020 8936 1122;
Website: www.laassociates.com

For local authority classes, consult your council or public library.

Conservation and restoration advice and information can also be sought from the following professional organizations:

The United Kingdom Institute for Conservation (UKIC),
109 The Chandlery, 50 Westminster Bridge Road,
London SE1 7QY, UK
Tel: 020 7721 8721; Fax: 020 7721 8722;
E-mail: ukic@ukic.org.uk

The American Institute for Conservation (AIC),
1717 K Street, NW, Suite 200, Washington, DC 20006, USA
Tel: 202 452 9545; Fax: 202 452 9328; E-mail: info@aic-faic.org

The International Institute for Conservation (IIC),
6 Buckingham Street, London WC2 6BA, UK
Tel: 020 7839 5975; Fax: 020 7976 1564;
E-mail: iicon@compuserve.com

Setting up a workshop

The first consideration when setting up a workshop is whether you are going to be employing or sharing the space with somebody else; if you are, it will need to have individual work areas as well as communal areas for certain treatments. Let us presume you are setting up on your own.

The ideal situation would be to design your workshop from scratch. However, it is most likely that you will be adapting an existing room that already has a window, electrics and possibly a sink with running water, and will have to design the layout around these features. If you are adapting a room in your own home, bear in mind that carpeting is not ideal for a workshop – apart from it presenting a fire risk, it could also sustain damage should you spill any chemicals, adhesives, and so on. You should choose some type of flooring that is non-slip and easily cleaned, such as vinyl tiles or linoleum. Ideally, it should also be chemical resistant. Ordinary curtains also present a fire risk; a metal-slatted blind would be a more suitable choice.

Furnishing and equipping a workshop is going to be a very expensive undertaking, so you need to think first about the essential large items when designing it. Health and safety should be considered from the start, so you need to allow space for an extraction unit, with or without a fume hood. Even if you are not going to be spraying resins you will need it for mixing and sanding adhesives and resins and working with chemicals. Next to or near this area you should have a metal cupboard for the storage of chemicals. A small refrigerator, though not essential, is a good place to store resins; the ice-making compartment is very useful for the overnight storage of mixed resins.

Your main work area will be the next thing to consider; try to position it near a window, as natural light (north, ideally) is most important for colour matching. If you do not have a window then lighting needs to be considered carefully. You will need to find lights that closely simulate daylight (Philips® produce some suitable types). You will also need a sink with running water for cleaning objects and equipment, and some containers of various sizes for the soaking of objects.

Have you got enough electrical power points? You will need several near your work area so that you can use a desk lamp and power tools. You will need a desk-top area for accepting and documenting objects. This would also be the logical place for your telephone and reference books. A permanent photographic area would be useful so that you do not have to keep setting up the backdrop and dismantling it all again. Cupboard space and shelving for storing materials and objects need to be carefully planned to ensure that you do not have to stretch over work surfaces – good planning makes for ease of working. Access to the workshop should also be considered – you may be asked to work on a large object. Do also give some thought to security, for you are likely to have numerous valuable objects on the premises. As well as fitting locks, bolts and a burglar alarm, make sure you and your clients have adequate insurance cover.

Having decided on the design of the fixed elements of your workshop you have to consider your equipment, tools and materials. If you are going to be spraying the next expensive items to buy will be an airbrush and a compressor. Other expensive larger items that are not essential but would be useful and could save you time are a steam cleaner, a binocular microscope and digital scales. A decent camera and lens to enable you to take detailed photographs, although not essential, is a very useful aid to documentation. Although you might have a standard vacuum cleaner for general cleaning, much more sensitive cleaners are available for object cleaning. They have narrow, flexible nozzles and a variable suction rate. Other useful items would be a hot-air blower or hair dryer, a set of balance scales and a tape dispenser.

Apart from the items already mentioned, the following is a list of the tools and equipment you may need:

Overalls	Micro-mesh® cloth
Dust mask	Garnet/glass papers
Fume mask	Dental wax
Gloves (nitrile/rubber)	Backing and moulding
Goggles	materials
Scalpel handle	Tapes
Cin bins (for sharps)	Saws
Scalpel blades (size 15)	Clamps
Spatulas (small and medium)	Cotton wool
Tweezers	Tissues
Pin-vice	Rolls of white paper towel
Files (needle and larger)	Tin foil
Dental tools	Clingfilm
Stencil brushes	Cork rings
Toothbrushes	Containers (for soaking
Photographic puffer	objects)
Level	Watch glasses
Paintbrushes	Glass bottles
Cocktail sticks	Glass beakers
Micro pipettes	Glass plate/ceramic tile
Pipettes (reusable glass)	Mixing bowls
Pipettes (disposable plastic)	Desiccator

Materials, manufacturers and suppliers

CLEANING

Ariel® or equivalent
From supermarkets

Synperonic® 91/6; Triton XL-80N in USA
Ellis Everard
Pine Street, South Bank Road,
Cargo Fleet,
Middlesborough TS3 8BD, UK
Tel: 01642 227388
Fax: 01642 220356

Conservator's Emporium
100 Standing Rock Circle,
Reno, NV 89511, USA
Tel: 775 852 0404
Fax: 775 852 3737

Laponite® R. D.
Rockwood Additives Ltd
PO Box 2, Moorfield Road,
Widnes, Ches. WA8 0JU, UK
Tel: 01514 952222

Stuart R. Stevenson
68 Clerkenwell Road, London
EC1M 5QA, UK
Tel: 020 7253 1693
Fax: 020 7490 0451

Conservation Resources LLC
8000-H Forbes Place,
Springfield, VA 22151, USA
Tel: 1 800 634 6932
Fax: 703 321 0629

Calgon®
*From supermarkets and
hardware stores*

Fisher Scientific
50 Fadem Road, Springfield,
NJ 07081, USA
Tel: 1 800 766 7000
From supermarkets

Groomstick®
Picreator Enterprises Ltd
44 Park View Gardens,
London NW4 2PN, UK
Tel: 020 8202 8972

Preservation Equipment Ltd
Shelfanger, Diss,
Norfolk IP22 2DG, UK
Tel: 01379 651527

Conservation Resources LLC
(*see above*)

Rowney kneadable putty rubber
Daler-Rowney Ltd
PO Box 10, Bracknell,
Berks. RG2 4ST, UK
From artists' suppliers

Conservation Resources LLC
(*see above*)

ACID-FREE BLOTTING PAPER

Falkiner Fine Papers Ltd
76 Southampton Row,
London WC1B 4AR, UK
Tel: 020 7831 1151

Conservation Resources LLC
(*see under Cleaning*)

ADHESIVES/RESINS

HMG®
H. Marcel Guest Ltd
Riverside Works,
Collyhurst Road,
Manchester M40 7RU, UK
Tel: 0161 2057631

Stuart R. Stevenson (*see under
Cleaning*)

Conservation Resources LLC
(*see under Cleaning*)

Paraloid® B72, Paraloid® B67
Rohm and Hass Ltd
Lennig House, 2 Masons Ave,
Croydon, Surrey CR9 3NB,
UK

Stuart R. Stevenson (*see under
Cleaning*)

Camlab Ltd
Nuffield Rd, Cambridge,
Cambs. CB4 1TH, UK
Tel: 01223 424222

Conservation Resources LLC
(*see under Cleaning*)

Paraloid® B99
Rohm and Hass Ltd (*see above*)

Epo-tek® 301
Conservation Resources Ltd
Units 1, 2, & 4, Pony Road,
Horspath Industrial Estate,
Cowley, Oxon. OX4 2RD,
UK
Tel: 01865 747755

Conservation Resources LLC
(*see under Cleaning*)

Hxtal® NYL-1
Conservator's Emporium (*see
under Cleaning*)

Stuart R. Stevenson (*see under
Cleaning*)

Araldite® 2020, also known as Ciba-Geigy® XW396/7
Ciba Polymers, Structural
Adhesives, Duxford,
Cambs. CB2 4QA, UK
Tel: 01223 832121
Fax: 01223 834404

Stuart R. Stevenson (*see under
Cleaning*)

Ciba Specialty Chemicals Corp.
Polymers Division, Formulated
Materials Group,
4917 Dawn Ave, E. Lansing,
MI 48823, USA
Tel: 517 351 5900
Fax: 517 351 9003

Fynebond®
Fyne Conservation Services
Airds Cottage, St Catherine's,
By Loch Fyne, Argyll PA25 8BA,
Scotland, UK

Stuart R. Stevenson (*see under
Cleaning*)

Araldite® 24hr, Araldite® rapid
Ciba Polymers (*see above*)
From hardware stores

Ciba Specialty Chemicals Corp.
(*see above*)

Super epoxy; equivalent to Devcon in USA
Plastic Padding Ltd
Wooburn Industrial Park,
Wooburn Green,
High Wycombe,
Bucks. HP1 0PE, UK
Tel: 01628 527912
From hardware stores

Conservation Resources LLC
(*see under Cleaning*)

Loctite® Super glue
Loctite UK Ltd
Welwyn Garden City,
Herts. AL7 1JB, UK
Tel: 01707 331277
From hardware stores

H. G. Pasternach
450 Nepperhan Ave, Yonkers,
NY, USA
Tel: 212 691 9555

Sebralit®
A. J. Lopez & Co. Ltd
Loco Residence, King's Cross
Goods Yard, York Way,
London N1 OAT, UK
Tel: 020 8544 9980

For an equivalent product in
the USA contact:
Superior Polyesters
Superior Adhesives, Inc.
1111 Godfrey Ave, Grand
Rapids, MI 49503, USA
or
Akemi Polyester
Jaeger & Condino, Inc.
PO Box 592,
35–44 61st Street, Woodside,
NY 11377, USA
Tel: 718 335 8300

FILLERS

Superfine casting plaster
The Fulham Pottery Ltd
8–10 Ingate Place, Battersea,
London SW8 3NS, UK

Fisher Scientific (*see under
Cleaning*)

Dental casting plaster
Clyman, Morells Barn,
Lagness, Chichester,
W. Sussex PO18 6LR, UK
Tel: 01243 265845

Darby Kent
25 Commerce Drive, Aston,
PA 19014, USA

Fine surface Polyfilla®
Polycell Products Ltd
Broadwater Road, Welwyn
Garden City,
Herts. AL7 3AZ, UK
Tel: 01707 328131
From hardware stores

Conservator's Emporium (*see
under Cleaning*)

**Modostuc® special surface
filler**
Plasveroi S.p.A
Via Camussone 38,
Frazione Giavenzano,
Vellezzo Bellini (PV), Italy
Tel: 0382 926895/057
Fax: 0382 926451

F.E.W.®
Bondaglass Voss Ltd
158–64 Ravenscroft Road,
Beckenham, Kent, UK
Tel: 020 8778 0071

Stuart R. Stevenson (*see under
Cleaning*)

For an equivalent product in
the USA contact:
Superior Polyesters
Superior Adhesives, Inc.
1111 Godfrey Ave, Grand
Rapids, MI 49503, USA
or
Akemi Polyester
Jaeger & Condino, Inc.
PO Box 592,
35–44 61st Street, Woodside,
NY 11377, USA
Tel: 718 335 8300

David's P38 Isopon®
W. David and Sons Ltd
Mnftg & Ind Chemists,
Dennington Ind. Estate,
Wellingborough,
Northants. NN8 2QP, UK
Tel: 01933 230330
From car repair shops

For an equivalent product in
the USA contact:
Superior Polyesters
Superior Adhesives, Inc.
1111 Godfrey Ave,
Grand Rapids, MI 49503, USA
or
Akemi Polyester
Jaeger & Condino, Inc.
PO Box 592,
35–44 61st Street, Woodside,
NY 11377, USA
Tel: 718 335 8300

Marine® Filler
Plastic Padding Ltd (*see under
Adhesives/resins*)
From car repair shops

For an equivalent product in
the USA contact:
Superior Polyesters
Superior Adhesives, Inc.
1111 Godfrey Ave, Grand
Rapids, MI 49503, USA
or
Akemi Polyester
Jaeger & Condino, Inc.
PO Box 592,
35–44 61st Street, Woodside,
NY 11377, USA
Tel: 718 335 8300

ICI white-cellulose stopper
Brown Brothers
6 Hemming St, London E1, UK
Tel: 020 7247 0591
From car repair shops

Milliput®
The Milliput Co.
Unit 5 The Marian, Dolgellau,
Mid Wales LL40 1UU, UK
Tel: 01341 422562

Stuart R. Stevenson (*see under
Cleaning*)

Conservation Resources LLC
(*see under Cleaning*)

**Trylon shallow-cast
embedding resin EM306 PA,
EM400 PA**
Trylon Ltd
Thrift Street, Wollaston,
Northants. NN9 7QS, UK
Tel: 01933 664275
Fax: 01933 664960

For an equivalent product in
the USA contact:
Superior Polyesters
Superior Adhesives, Inc.
1111 Godfrey Ave, Grand
Rapids, MI 49503, USA
or
Akemi Polyester
Jaeger & Condino, Inc.
PO Box 592,
35–44 61st Street, Woodside,
NY 11377, USA
Tel: 718 335 8300

Sylmasta® A + B
Hobby Aids/Sylmasta
PO Box 262, Haywards Heath,
W. Sussex RH16 3FR, UK
Tel: 01444 415027

Araldite® AY 103,HY 965
Ciba Polymers (*see under
Adhesives/resins*)

Stuart R. Stevenson (*see under
Cleaning*)

Ciba Specialty Chemicals Corp.
(*see under Adhesives/resins*)

Araldite® 2011
Ciba Polymers (*see under
Adhesives/resins*)

Ciba Specialty Chemicals Corp.
(*see under Adhesives/resins*)

MOULDING MATERIALS

Dental wax
Elite Wax
Toughened modelling wax,
Wright Cottrell
Kingsway West,
Dundee DD2 3QD, UK
Tel: 01382 833866
Fax: 01382 811042

Darby Kent (*see under Fillers*)

Silcoset® 105/hardener A
Ambersil Ltd
Wylds Road, Castlefield
Industrial Estate, Bridgewater,
Som. TA6 4DD, UK
Tel: 01278 424200

Indestructible Paint, Inc.
66 Erna Avenue, Milford,
CT 064460, USA

Provil®, Optosil®
Heraeus Kulzer
Heraeus House, Albert Rd,
Northbrook St, Newbury,
Berks. RG 14 1DL, UK
Tel: 01635 30500

Heraeus Kulzer, Inc.
99 Business Park Drive,
Armonk, NY 10504, USA

Elite® Double
Zhermack
Via Bovazecchino 100,
45021 Badia, Polesine
(Rovigo), Italy
Tel: 0425 53595

Ivoclar
Meridian South, Meridian
Business Centre,
Leicester LE19 2DY, UK
Tel & Fax: 01162 654056

**Coltene® Rapid (similar to
Optosil®)**
Coltene/Whaledent Ltd
The President Suite-C,
Kendal House, Victoria Way,
Burgess Hill, Sussex RH15
9NF, UK
Tel: 01444 235486
Fax: 01444 870640

Coltene/Whaledent Inc.
750 Corporate Drive, Mawah,
NJ 07430, USA
Tel: 201 512 8000

Latex rubber
Trylon Ltd (*see under Fillers*)

Conservation Resources (*see
under Cleaners*)

Plasticine
From artists' suppliers

Plastiline®
Jacobson Chemical Ltd
Jacobson House,
The Crossways, Churt,
Surrey GU10 2J0, UK
Tel: 01428 713637
Fax: 01428 712835

Block wax
Alec Tiranti Ltd
27 Warren Street,
London W1P 5DG, UK
Tel: 020 7636 8565

Conservator's Emporium (*see under Cleaning*)

Vaseline®
From supermarkets & chemists

BULKING AGENTS

Micro balloons
Freeman Distributors
Unit 2, 1st Avenue, Blue Bridge
Industrial Estate, Halstead,
Essex CO9 9EX, UK
Tel: 01787 472300

3M Scotchlite Bubbles
3M Center Building 22-8c-04,
St Paul, MN 55144, USA
Tel: 1 888 364 3577

Glass beads
Freeman Distributors (*see above*)

Fine Industrial Associates
1891 Grand Avenue, Baldwin,
NY 11510, USA

Cab-O-sil® M5
Merck Eurolab
VWR International Ltd
Merck House, Pool,
Dorset BH15 1TD, UK

Conservation Materials, Ltd
240 Freeport Blvd, Box 2884,
Sparks, NV 89431, USA
Tel: 702 331 0582

Aerosil® R805
Degussa AG
GB AC, Postfach 110533,
D-6000, Frankfurt 11,
Germany

Conservation Materials, Ltd
(*see above*)

Gasil® 23c matting agent
Stuart R. Stevenson (*see under Cleaning*)

Conservation Resources LLC
(*see under Cleaning*)

Vermiculite
Dupré Ltd
Southern Camworth Road,
Hertford, Herts. SG13 7DL, UK
Tel: 01992 582541
From hardware stores

Aldrich Chemical Company,
Inc.
PO Box 2060, Milwaukee,
WI 53201, USA
Tel: 1 800 558 9160

PAINTING MEDIUMS AND PAINTS

Rowney Cryla colours and acrylic mediums
Daler-Rowney Ltd (*see under Cleaning*)

Daler-Rowney Ltd
12 Percy St, London W1A 2BP,
UK
Fax: 020 7580 7534

Liquitex® acrylic artist colours and acrylic mediums
Binney and Smith, Inc.
Easton, PA 18044-0431, USA
From artists' suppliers

Golden® acrylic colours and acrylic mediums
Golden Artists Colors, Inc.
188 Bell Road, New Berlin,
NY, NY 13411, USA
Tel: 607 847 6154
Fax: 607 847 6767
From artists' suppliers

Sylmasta® Coldglaze System
Hobby Aids/Sylmasta (*see under Fillers*)

Winsor & Newton®/dry ground pigments
From artists' suppliers

Al Friedman
44 W. 18th Street, NY,
NY 10011, USA
Tel: 212 243 9000

Maimeri® restoration colours
Maimeri pigments
F.lli Maimeri & Co. Srl
Medigia (Mi), Italy

Stuart R. Stevenson (*see under Cleaning*)

Talas
568 Broadway, NY,
NY 10012, USA
Tel: 212 219 2394

Kremer® pigments
A. P. Fitzpatrick
Fine Art Materials
1 Barnabas Studios,
10–22 Barnabas Road,
London E9 5SB, UK
Tel: 020 8985 7865/7669
Fax: 020 8985 7659

Kremer
228 Elizabeth St, NY,
NY 10012, USA
Tel: 212 219 2394

Porcelain Restoration Glaze
Golden Artist Colors, Inc. (*see above*)

Stuart R. Stevenson (*see under Cleaning*)

Polyester pastes
Trylon Ltd (*see under Fillers*)

For an equivalent product in
the USA contact:
Superior Polyesters
Superior Adhesives, Inc.
1111 Godfrey Ave, Grand
Rapids, MI 49503, USA
or
Akemi Polyester
Jaeger & Condino, Inc.
PO Box 592,
35–44 61st Street, Woodside,
NY 11377, USA

Araldite® colouring epoxy paste
Ciba Polymers (*see under Adhesives/resins*)

Ciba Specialty Chemicals Corp.
(*see under Adhesives/resins*)

Rustin's® Plastic Coating
Rustin's Ltd
Waterloo Road,
London NW2 7TY, UK
Tel: 020 8450 4666

Stuart R. Stevenson (*see under Cleaning*)

Gold leaf loose/transfer, gold powder, bronzing powders, gold size, etc
L. Cornelissen & Son Ltd
105 Great Russell Street,
London WC1B 3RY, UK
Tel: 020 7636 1045

Stuart R. Stevenson (*see under Cleaning*)

Pear Paint
308 Canal Street, NY,
NY 10013, USA
Tel: 212 431 7932

FINISHING MATERIALS

Micro-mesh® cloth/files
Micro Surface Finishing
Products, Inc.
Box 818, Wilton,
Iowa 52778, USA
Tel: 319 732 3240
Fax: 319 732 3390

P. W. Products Ltd
64–6 High Street, Barnet,
Herts. EN5 5SJ, UK

Abrasive papers/garnet papers
From hardware stores

Grainger
360 W. 31st Street, NY,
NY 10011-2727, USA
Tel: 212 629 5660

Solvol Aurosol® polish
Solvolene Lubricants
22 Reginald Square,
London SE8 4RX,
UK
Tel: 020 8692 2241
From hardware stores

Renaissance® Wax
Picreator Renaissance Products
(*see under Cleaning*)

Conservation Resources LLC
(*see under Cleaning*)

Prelim® metal polish
Picreator Renaissance Products
(*see under Cleaning*)

Conservation Resources LLC (*see under Cleaning*)

Greygate® plastic polish
Greygate Chemical Products Ltd
Fir Tree Lane, Groby, Leics., UK

Stuart R. Stevenson (*see under Cleaning*)

CHEMICALS

Acetone
Merck Eurolab (*see under Bulking agents*)

Stuart R. Stevenson (*see under Cleaning*)
For small amounts

Fisher Scientific (*see under Cleaning*)

Industrial methylated spirits (IMS)
Merck Eurolab (*see under Bulking agents*)

Fisher Scientific (*see under Cleaning*)

Hydrogen peroxide
Merck Eurolab (*see under Bulking agents*)

Fisher Scientific (*see under Cleaning*)

White spirit
Merck Eurolab (*see under Bulking agents*)
From hardware stores

Ammonia
Merck Eurolab (*see under Bulking agents*)

Fisher Scientific (*see under Cleaning*)

Dichloromethane
Merck Eurolab (*see under Bulking agents*)

Fisher Scientific (*see under Cleaning*)

Nitromors®; Rock Miracle in USA
Wilcot Decorative Products Co. Ltd
Alexandra Park,
Bristol BS16 2BQ, UK
Tel: 01272 653256
From hardware stores

Auro Paint Stripping Paste
AURO Planzenchemie GmbH
D-38122 Braunschweig, Germany
Tel: 0531 895086
or
Unit 1, Goldstones Farm, Ashdon, Saffron Walden, Essex CB10 2LZ, UK
Tel: 01799 584888

3M Paint and Varnish Remover
3M UK plc
Hudson Road,
Beds. MK41 0HR, UK
Tel: 01234 229420

Douglas Kane Ltd,
Carlyon Road, Atherstone, War. CU9 1LQ, UK
From some hardware stores

Sylmasta® Thinners SL146
Hobby Aids/Sylmasta (*see under Fillers*)

Frigilene®, Ercalene®
H. S. Walsh & Sons Ltd
21 St Cross Street,
Hatton Garden, London
EC1N 8UN, UK
Tel: 020 7242 3711
Fax: 020 7242 3712

Conservation Resources (UK) Ltd (*see under Adhesives/resins*)

Conservation Resources LLC (*see under Cleaning*)

Jenolite® (rust stabilizer); equivalent to Naval Jelly in USA
Duckhams Oil Ltd
157–9 Mason Hill, Bromley, Kent BR2 9HU, UK
From hardware stores in USA

SUPPORT MATERIALS

3M Scotch® Magic® Tape Sellotape®
Scotch Commercial Markets Group
3M UK plc
PO Box 1, Bracknell, Berks., UK
From stationers & hardware stores

Masking tape
J. W. Bollom & Co. Ltd
PO Box 78, Croydon Road, Beckenham,
Kent BR3 4BL, UK
Tel: 020 8658 2299
From stationers & hardware stores

X-Lite®
Orthopaedic Systems
Unit G22/23, Oldgate, Michael's Industrial Estate, Widnes, Ches. WA8 8TL, UK
Tel: 01514 203250

E. B. I. Medical Systems, Inc.
NJ, USA
Tel: 937 299 9300

Berna assemblers
Hardi
89/91 High Street, Rickmansworth,
Herts. WD3 1EF, UK
Tel: 01923 774134

Stuart R. Stevenson (*see under Cleaning*)

End-crack clamp
B. Hart (Luthiers tools)
24 Ann Street, Gadlys, Aberdare, Mid Glam.
CF44 8DU, UK
Tel: 01685 886004

G clamps
Buck and Ryan
101 Tottenham Court Rd, London W1P ODY, UK
Tel: 020 7636 7485
From hardware stores

Harbor Freight Tools
3491 Mission Oaks Blvd, Camarillo, CA 93011-6010, USA
Tel: 1 800 423 2567

TOOLS AND EQUIPMENT

Stencil brushes
High Peak Brushes Ltd
Mill Street, Glossop, Derby.
SK13 8PT, UK
From artists' suppliers

Al Friedman (*see under Painting mediums and paints*)

Paint brushes (sable)
From artists' suppliers

Al Friedman (*see under Painting mediums and paints*)

Micro pipettes
Camlab Ltd (*see under Adhesives/resins*)

Fisher Scientific (*see under Cleaning*)

Glass pipettes and teats
Merck Eurolab (*see under Bulking agents*)

Fisher Scientific (*see under Cleaning*)

Disposable plastic pipettes
Camlab Ltd (*see under Adhesives/resins*)

Fisher Scientific (*see under Cleaning*)

Scalpel blades
Swann-Morton Ltd
Sheffield SB6 2BJ, UK
From artists' suppliers

Merck Eurolab (*see under Bulking agents*)

Conservation Resources LLC (*see under Cleaning*)

Metal spatulas, files, rifflers, dental tools, etc
Alec Tiranti Ltd (*see under Moulding materials*)

Conservation Resources LLC (*see under Cleaning*)

Glass bottles
Aldrich Chemicals Co.
Ltd
The Old Brick Yard,
New Road, Gillingham,
Dorset SP8 4JL, UK
Tel: 01747 822211

Fisher Scientific (*see under Cleaning*)

Screw-top jars
Merck Eurolab (*see under Bulking agents*)

Fisher Scientific (*see under Cleaning*)

Hand-held hot-air blower
Elton Systems Ltd
Unit 2, Verulam Industrial
Estate, London Road,
St Albans, Herts. AL1 1JB,
UK
Tel: 01727 40266

Grainger (*see under Finishing materials*)

Steam cleaner (Derotor Models GV & GV6)
The John Quayle Dental
Manufacturing Co. Ltd
Derotor House,
Dominion Way, Worthing,
W. Sussex BN14 8QN, UK
Tel: 01903 204427/8/9

Grainger (*see under Finishing materials*)

UV Light equipment
Macam Photometrics Ltd
10 Kelvin Square, Livingston
EH54 5PF Scotland, UK
Tel: 01506 437391

Fisher Scientific (*see under Cleaning*)

Overhead laboratory lighting
Philips Lighting Ltd
420/430 London Rd,
Croydon CR9 3QR, UK
Tel: 020 8665 6655

Fisher Scientific (*see under Cleaning*)

Bench and Anglepoise lamps
C.L.E. Design Ltd
69–71 Haydens Road,
Wimbledon,
London SW19 1HQ,
UK
Tel: 020 8540 5772

Tudor Electric
222 East 46th St, NY,
NY 10017, USA
Tel: 212 867 7550

Digital scales
Philip Harris Scientific
6/8 Western Avenue, Park
Royal, London W3 OTE,
UK
Tel: 020 8992 5555
Fax: 020 8993 8020

Ohaus Scale Corporation
Florham Park, NJ 07932,
USA

Desiccators
Philip Harris Scientific (*see above*)

Fisher Scientific (*see under Cleaning*)

Cork rings
Philip Harris Scientific (*see above*)

Fisher Scientific (*see under Cleaning*)

Microscopes
Kyowa
7-1, 1-Chome, Tamagawa,
Chofu-shi, Tokyo, Japan

Euromicrovision Co. Ltd
Finlay House, Southfields
Road, Kineton Road
Industial Estate,
Southam, War. CV47 0FB,
UK
Tel: 01926 813043
Fax: 01926 817186

Carl Zeiss
1 Zeiss Drive, Thornwood,
NY 10597, USA

Morrell
502 Walt Whitman Road,
Melville, NY 11747-2112,
USA

Watch glasses
Camlab Ltd (*see under Adhesives/resins*)

Fisher Scientific (*see under Cleaning*)

Banding wheel
The Fulham Pottery (*see under Fillers*)

Ceramic Supply
Sculpture House,
100 Camp Meeting Ave,
Skillman, NJ 08558,
USA

Airbrushes/compressors/ extraction units
The Airbrush and Spray Centre
39 Littlehampton Road,
Worthing, W. Sussex
BN13 1QJ, UK
Tel: 01903 26691

Paasche Airbrush Company
7440 West Lawrence Ave,
Harwood Heights,
IL 60656-3412, USA

Dust/fume masks
3M House
Market House, Bracknell,
Berks. RG12 1JU, UK
Tel: 01344 426726
or
3 Parr Road, Stanmore, Mddx
HA7 1PZ, UK
Tel: 020 8381 1811

Fisher Scientific (*see under Cleaning*)

Nitrile gloves
Sentinel Laboratories Ltd
Mitchell House, Ilfield,
Crawley, W. Sussex
RH11 0AQ, UK
Tel: 01293 526457

Conservation Resources LLC
(*see under Cleaning*)

Roll towels, clingfilm, kitchen foil, tissues, vinyl gloves
Alpha Supplies
92–108 Cheshire Street,
London E2 6EJ, UK
From supermarkets

Laboratory sealing film
Whatmans Labsales Ltd
20/22 St Leonards Road,
Maidstone, Kent ME16 0LS,
UK

Fisher Scientific (*see under Cleaning*)

Melinex®
Film Sales Ltd
145 Nathan Way,
Woolwich Industrial Estate,
London SE28 0BE, UK
Tel: 020 8311 2000

Conservation Resources LLC
(*see under Cleaning*)

Polyethylene foams
Pentonville Rubber Ltd
104–6 Pentonville Road,
London N1 9JB, UK
Tel: 020 7837 7553
Fax: 020 7278 7392

Fisher Scientific (*see under Cleaning*)

Tin plate
W. L. Cooke Ltd
Cookes Corner, Wange Road,
Chadwell Heath,
Essex RH6 4BW, UK

Reading list

The inclusion of a title in this list does not necessarily imply a recommendation of the techniques advocated.

RESTORATION/ CONSERVATION

Lesley Acton and Paul McAuley, *Repairing Pottery and Porcelain: A Practical Guide*, Herbert Press, 1996

Jean-Michel Andre, *The Restorer's Handbook of Ceramics and Glass*, Van Nostrand Reinhold, 1976

Susan Buys and Victoria Oakley, *The Conservation and Restoration of Ceramics*, Butterworth-Heinemann, 1993

Judith Larney, *Restoring Ceramics*, Barrie and Jenkins, 1975 (2nd edn 1978)

C. S. M. Parsons and F. H. Curl, *China Mending and Restoration*, Faber, 1963

H. J. Plenderleith and A. E. A. Werner, *The Conservation of Antiquities and Works of Art*, Oxford University Press, 1971 (2nd edn)

Susan Wells, *Mend Your Own China and Glass*, Bell, 1975

M. White, *Restoring Fine China*, Batsford, 1981

TECHNOLOGY AND ART HISTORY

John Ayers, Oliver Impey and J. V. G. Mallet, *Porcelain for Palaces: The Fashion for Japan in Europe 1650–1750*, Oriental Ceramic Society, 1990

Peter Bradshaw, *18th century English Porcelain Figures 1745–1795*, Antique Collectors' Club Ltd, 1981

William Chaffers, *Concise Marks and Monograms on Pottery and Porcelain*, Wordsworth Editions, 1989 (2nd edn 1990)

B. H. Charles, *Pottery and Porcelain: A Glossary of Terms*, Hippocrene Books, 1974

David Harris Cohen and Catherine Hess, *Looking at European Ceramics*, Getty/ British Museum Press, 1993

A. W. Coysh, *Blue Printed Earthenware 1800–1850*, David and Charles, 1972

A. W. Coysh, *Blue and White Transfer Ware 1780–1840*, David and Charles, 1974

A. A. Eaglestone and T. A. Lockett, *The Rockingham Pottery*, David and Charles, 1973

Ian Freestone and David Gaimster (eds), *Pottery in the Making: World Ceramic Traditions*, British Museum Press, 1997

G. A. Godden, *Encyclopaedia of British Pottery and Porcelain Marks*, Herbert Jenkins, 1964

G. A. Godden, *Godden's Guide to English Porcelain*, Granada Publishing, 1978

R. Haggar and E. Adams, *Mason Porcelain and Ironstone 1796–1853*, Faber, 1977 (1st edn)

F. Hamer, *The Potter's Dictionary of Materials and Techniques*, Pitman, 1977

Jessica Harrison-Hall, *Catalogue of Late Yuan and Ming Ceramics in the British Museum*, British Museum Press, 2001

R. L. Hobson, *Catalogue of the Frank Lloyd Collection of Worcester Porcelain of the Wall Period*, British Museum, 1925

W. B. Honey, *English Pottery and Porcelain*, A. and C. Black, 1975 (6th edn)

W. B. Honey, *Old English Porcelain*, Faber, 1977 (3rd edn)

Heather Lawrence, *The Castleford Pottery Pattern Book 1796*, EP Publishing Ltd, 1973

Heather Lawrence, *Yorkshire Pots and Potteries*, David and Charles, 1972

T. A. Lockett, *Davenport Pottery and Porcelain 1794–1887*, David and Charles, 1972

Margaret Medley, *The Chinese Potter*, Phaidon, 1976

G. W. Rhead and F. A. Rhead, *Staffordshire Pots and Potters*, EP Publishing Ltd, 1977

Daniel Rhodes, *Clay and Glazes for the Potter*, Pitman, 1973

Daniel Rhodes, *Stoneware and Porcelain: The Art of High Fired Pottery*, Pitman, 1960

H. Sandon, *Worcester Porcelain 1751–1793*, Barrie and Jenkins, 1974

H. M. Saunders, *The World of Japanese Ceramics*, Kodansha International, 1976

George Savage, *Porcelain Through the Ages*, Penguin Books, 1954

George Savage and Harold Newman, *An Illustrated Dictionary of Ceramics*

Geoge Savage and Harold Newman with John Cushion, *Introductory List of European Factories and their Marks*, Thames and Hudson, 1974 (2nd edn 1976)

A. Smith, *Liverpool Herculaneum Pottery*, Barrie and Jenkins, 1970

Mention must also be made of the Faber Monographs on pottery and porcelain. Well over thirty titles have been published, although many are now out of print. They should be available through a good lending library.

Glossary

The definitions listed here relate specifically to the meaning of the words as they are used in this book.

alum
Double sulphate of aluminium and potassium.

amine
Compound formed from ammonia.

banding wheel
Free-spinning, balanced, weighted wheel.

biscuit-ware
Ceramic after first firing, before glazing.

bitumen
Natural hydrocarbon; mineral pitch.

bone china
Translucent ceramic in the making of which calcined bone is added to the clay.

Bow
English, eighteenth-century, soft-paste porcelain.

calcined
Chemically changed by burning.

celadon
Type of green glaze ranging in colour from putty to sea green.

celadon ware
Chinese or Korean ceramic with a celadon glaze. The decoration is usually incised.

censers
Vessels for burning incense.

Chelsea
English, eighteenth-century, soft-paste porcelain.

colloid
In suspension, gel-like.

congee
Water in which rice has been boiled.

cross-linking
Chemical reaction that occurs in polymers, where new, strong bonds are formed between the molecules; very difficult to reverse.

Delft ware
Sixteenth- and seventeenth-century tin-glazed earthenware.

desiccator
Airtight vessel in which a solvent can be evaporated; used to dismantle objects.

earthenware
Fired, porous pottery; can be glazed or unglazed.

enamel
Vitrified coating, transparent or opaque, applied to ceramics or metals.

enamelling
Applying enamels to a fired glaze and refiring at a lower temperature in order to fuse them to the glaze.

enzyme
Protein acting as a catalyst in a specific biochemical reaction.

exothermic
Producing heat as the result of a chemical reaction.

fettling
Removing or trimming excess material along seams of moulds.

gilding
Liquid gold or gold leaf applied to the fired glaze and refired at a low temperature just sufficient to fuse it to the glaze.

gum ammoniac
Resin made from the thickened juice of an umbelliferous plant.

gum mastic
Type of adhesive made from resin exuded by the mastic tree.

gum of Chios
See gum mastic.

hard-paste porcelain
High-fired, non-porous, translucent ceramic.

ionic (of a detergent)
Containing electrically charged particles.

isinglass
Type of gelatin made from the air bladder of the sturgeon fish, used as an adhesive.

Iznik ware
Sixteenth- and seventeenth-century type of Turkish, decorated, glazed earthenware.

jollying
Process of making pots in a revolving mould using a template to push the clay into shape.

jollying arm
Attachment to a potter's wheel housing on to which a template is fixed for jollying.

kaolin
China clay, used in the making of porcelain and as a bulking agent for fillers.

kolinsky
Semi-aquatic mink found in eastern Asia, closely related to the weasel.

Kuan ware (Guan ware)
Imperial ware of the Southern Sung dynasty, generally dark-bodied with a thick, opaque, crackle glaze.

micro-balloons
Minute spheres made of phenolic resin or glass having the appearance of fine white powder.

microcrystalline
Of minute crystals.

overglaze (of decoration)
Applied to the glaze before firing.

oxide
A compound of oxygen and some other element or radical.

oxidize
To introduce oxygen.

pad-saw
Versatile G-shaped saw with a flat, removable blade.

Parian ware
Nineteenth-century, English, high-fired, non-porous, unglazed ceramic.

piercing-saw
G-shaped saw with fine, removable blades to enable pierced work.

Plastazote®
Polyethylene foam in the form of sheets.

plasticizer
Substance added to a material to make it less brittle.

poulticing
Extraction by means of a poultice (absorbent material).

relative humidity
Relationship between the temperature and the amount of moisture in the atmosphere.

sable
Tail hairs of a species of weasel from the cold climates of Russia.

soft-paste porcelain
Slightly porous, opaque ceramic, fired at a lower temperature than hard-paste.

stoneware
Dense, vitrified, high-fired ceramic; may be glazed or unglazed.

string drill
Drill consisting of a weighted flywheel pierced by a central rod. A spade bit in a drill chuck is attached to the bottom end of the rod; string runs through a hole in the top of the rod and is attached to either end of the crossbar positioned above the flywheel. Spinning the flywheel or the crossbar winds the string around the rod and causes the crossbar to rise. Downwards pressure on the crossbar will spin the positioned bit. Stored energy in the flywheel will automatically cause the cycle to reverse, so that the drill is rotating alternately clockwise and anticlockwise. The modern version of this device is known as a watchmaker's drill.

talc
Magnesium silicate.

thixotropic
Showing a temporary reduction in viscosity when shaken or stirred.

tin snips
Shears bladed like those of pliers, designed for cutting tin sheet metal.

Ting ware (Ding ware)
Thin, white porcelain with transparent, ivory-toned glaze, made in the Song and Yuan dynasties. The name derives from Ting-chou in northern China, where it was first produced. The decoration is either carved into the body at the leather-hard stage or moulded.

titanium dioxide
Pure white powder of high opacity, used especially as a pigment.

transfer
Enamel paint printed by lithography on to paper that has been faced with a gelatinous coating. The design is transferred to the ceramic by first coating the ware with a resin, the transfer is rubbed on and the paper removed. The ceramic is then refired at a lower temperature, just enough to fuse the enamel to the glaze and burn off the resin.

underglaze (of decoration)
Applied to the ceramic body before the glaze.

vermiculite
Lightweight, water-absorbent particles made from mica (a rock-forming mineral) expanded by heat.

viscosity
Semi-liquid or glutinous state.

wasters
Objects damaged during firing.

watch glass
Curved glass dish used in laboratories to hold small quantities of a substance.

water white
Translucent in finish.

Wedgwood
Eighteenth-century stoneware made in Staffordshire.

whiting
Calcium carbonate.

X-lite®
Open-cell bandage of polyester mixed with inorganic filler.

zinc oxide
Whitish, solid, natural mineral used as a flux in glazes and as a paint pigment.

Index